URBAN SHOTS
DOWN THE ROAD

Ahmed Faiyaz grew up in Bangalore (now Bengaluru) and now lives in Dubai. He's a book and film addict, and apart from reading books and watching cinemas of all genres, he is a passionate writer. He is the bestselling author of *Love, Life & all that Jazz*, *Another Chance* and *Scammed*, and the editor of *Urban Shots: Crossroads*. He has written six short films and two feature films, including *Graveyard Shift*, based on his novella by the same name.

Rohini Kejriwal is a freelance writer, photographer and curator from Calcutta. She is always up for a good story, travelling, new music, strong coffee and the company of crows. A self-proclaimed beauty hunter, she curates her own daily newsletter of art, poetry and music called *The Alipore Post* (www.thealiporepost.com).

URBAN SHOTS
DOWN THE ROAD

Edited by
Ahmed Faiyaz
& Rohini Kejriwal

RUPA

Published by
Rupa Publications India Pvt. Ltd 2015
7/16, Ansari Road, Daryaganj
New Delhi 110002

Sales centres:
Allahabad Bengaluru Chennai
Hyderabad Jaipur Kathmandu
Kolkata Mumbai

ISBN: 978-81-291-3799-9

First impression 2015

10 9 8 7 6 5 4 3 2 1

Contents

Foreword   ix
Sahil Khan

Attendance is Compulsory

Down the Road   3
Ahmed Faiyaz

Rishi and Me: A Love Story   16
Ira Trivedi

Knockout   25
Ahmed Faiyaz

Sororicide   35
Paritosh Uttam

Reason   44
Ahmed Faiyaz

The Music Room   48
Ira Trivedi

Welcome to St. Gibbs   57
Ahmed Faiyaz

Smells Like Home   62
Aashish Mehrotra

One Bump Does No Harm   73
Naman Saraiya

That's It?   79
Sahil Khan

Festivals, Elections & Placements

Loves Me, Loves Me Not   85
Vibha Batra

Well-placed   89
Ahmed Faiyaz

The Café with No Name   99
Sneh Thakur

Between Friends   107
Paritosh Uttam

Dimples and Cute Smiles   113
Ranjani Muthu

One and One Eleven   122
Prateek Gupta

Setting   138
Ahmed Faiyaz

Lights Out

Just a Moment   159
Nikhil Rajagopalan

Learning and Unlearning   166
Rohini Kejriwal

The Worm That Turned   172
Malathi Jaikumar

Bellow Yellow   182
Chinmayi Bali

Dare to Bare   185
Malathi Jaikumar

Fresher   191
Sneh Thakur

Looking Back

Strangers in Strange Places   203
Abhijit Bhaduri

Time   206
Ahmed Faiyaz

Remember Me?   212
Ahmed Faiyaz

An Accidental Start   217
Kunal Dhabalia

Growing Up   224
Rohini Kejriwal

Essays

Fiction on Campus   231
Sonia Safri

Bollywood on Campus   235
Aseem Rastogi

Foreword

SAHIL KHAN

School and college—for some people a wonderful experience, for some a painful journey they want to erase from their memory. Nevertheless, they're always the most remembered times of our lives because they formed the foundation of what we aspired to, and what we were to become.

Trying to ensure we had at least the minimum possible attendance and passing grade, cracking jokes in the class, bunking with friends, and troubling teachers or professors—all of this, I imagine, defined our student lives. Like they say, 'If you haven't done it, you haven't been there.'

Though the atmosphere has more or less been the same, a quick comparison of what Gen-X and Gen-Y have experienced on campus shows how times change. Today, 10-year-olds come home talking about girlfriends and boyfriends, and try to find answers as to which hobby elective they should go for—not bothering with what their peers or parents would say. Twenty years ago, making choices was simpler. You did as the crowd did or as the parents decided. Isn't that how you ended up in the engineering college? Or was it the medical school?

Movies are a reflection of a society which is yet to welcome a thought with open arms, and it is these movies that make the society more comfortable with a certain idea. The 1992 hit, *Jo Jeeta Wohi Sikandar*, though primarily focused on the competition between the hero and villain, had college love and politics entwined with the plot. In comparison, 2009's *Wake Up Sid* was less about college love and more about youth trying to carve an identity for themselves. But I believe the most courageous move was taken on the small screen with *Just Mohabbat,* which first aired in 1996. Amongst the saas-bahu serials, wrestling and cartoons, and the sometimes relatable *The Wonder Years,* this show chronicling a boy's growing years, from school to college, his friends, even an imaginary one, and his school crush, was definitely a first for the Indian drawing rooms.

The transition from school to college would've been a culture shock for many, mostly because we would have moved away from the closed environment of our homes for the first time.

Our experiences from school and back home were the factors affecting our choices unconsciously. And it is those choices that made us who we are today—in how we choose our friends, our career path and our life partner.

In the stories that follow, we'll take a walk down the lives and experiences on campus—some jovial, while others painfully heart-wrenching—through the changing times.

Attendance is Compulsory

Down the Road

AHMED FAIYAZ

Boman Baltiwala doodled with rapt attention, lost in his dreams as Professor Bhaskar Raj, popularly known as Bouncer, worked out the answer to an accounting problem on the blackboard. Abid Samar peeked into his notebook, wondering what he was drawing so furiously.

'Tubby, why aren't you copying down what Bouncer is writing on the board? Come on dude, start copying it.'

Abid was his best friend and also the only one in class who bullied him. Tubby, apart from being a cartoonist, also sang and danced well and could imitate anybody in class. The fact that he weighed over 90 kilos made his impressions even more animated.

'Why don't you copy it? I'll take it down from you later,' he said, licking his lips and focussing all his attention on the sketch.

'I would, if I could see as far as the blackboard,' Abid said, squinting to try and make out the workings on the board.

'Get a pair of glasses, bugger,' Tubby said without looking up.

'Nah, Sunaina doesn't like me wearing glasses. She thinks guys who wear glasses are nerdy.'

'Get contact lens then.'

'It's too much of a hassle man! Put them on every morning; take them off, pain in the backside. The only thing I can't see is the damn blackboard.'

'Hmm...'

'What the fuck are you drawing?'

'I'll show you later.'

'You've become a crazy guy man. You haven't imitated Bouncer in days. You've been disappearing right after school. You don't hang out with us…'

'I'm okay bugger, I'm just going home and studying.' Studying was what least interested him, as he topped the class every trimester—from the bottom.

'Chal let's have some fun. Imitate Bouncer.'

'No bugger, not now.'

'I'll tear up your work of art you tubby Picasso!'

'Okay, okay.' He cleared his throat, and slouched behind Arpit. 'Aye ples take out youver notebook and do the sum haan. Yes, wokay, haan you only,' Tubby said in a nasal twang with a lisp, at which the rest of the class erupted in laughter.

Bouncer turned around with a mad look on his face. Ajay and Mohit in the row behind them were in splits.

He loosened his tie and removed his collar button before rolling up his sleeves. His blood pressure began to rise and he turned around with a barmy look in his eyes. Students in every other class were terrified of him, it was only this batch that mocked and ridiculed him. He paced up and down the row, staring at everyone with suspicion.

'Aye, the four of you, ples stand up haan. Ajay, I'm telling you haan. Yes, you, you and you also. Bring youver books here,' he said.

The four of them reluctantly walked up to him. 'I know it's one of you haan. One day, I'll catch that fellow and give him a thrashing,' he said, turning his gaze from one to the other, while all four of them stared at the ground.

'Sir, I forgot my book,' Ajay said, at which he was rudely pushed out of class with his Walkman. He had been busy listening to *Actor* by MLTR. He walked out and, turning the tape to the other side, started playing *Phenomenon* by LL Cool J. In class or outside made no difference to him.

'I didn't quite understand the workings, sir. I was waiting for you to finish, I wanted to ask a question, before I copied it,' Mohit explained, quite convincingly.

'Aye, yes ples, get out I say.' He turned his gaze to Abid, looking at him suspiciously. 'So this is your notebook haan? I don't see any workings, only your signature all over the top margin. Get out of class,' he said, before Abid could explain.

'And you, mixing with these rascals haan? Aye what have you done?' he asked, snatching Tubby's notebook, while Tubby held on to it tightly. 'What is this? A sketch of a girl, haan? Is this what I was doing on the blackboard? Get out I say, aye please go...'

As the rest of the class leaned forward to try and see what he had drawn, Bouncer raised Tubby's notebook towards the class.

'So, who is the babe?' Abid asked outside the classroom.

'Yes, tell us you fat tub,' Ajay said. 'Thanks to you we've been thrown out again. This sucks!'

'Speak up, or you won't get any of my homemade lunch today,' Mohit said. Mohit's lunch box was what inspired Tubby to drag himself to school every morning.

'I don't know. She is from Shepherd's Girls. I don't know her name, I just see her every day when I walk down to my Dad's office,' Tubby said nervously.

'From Shepherd's? He's bullshitting. I would have known by now,' Ajay said while the rest ignored him.

'This is why he runs away right after school,' Abid said, pushing his long hair back with one hand.

'Ahaan this is interesting! She's quite a stunner, isn't she Abid? She is your imaginary girlfriend?' Mohit asked, almost tearing off the page.

'Of course not, she's a real person,' Tubby said.

'There's only one way to know. Show us,' Mohit said.

'Guys stop this right now; I can't do that, not with her. I'm in love with this girl,' Tubby said, wiping sweat off his brow.

'Right, this guy is making it up,' Abid said. 'Dude, if this was the case we would have noticed her. I haven't seen anyone like her.' Mohit and Ajay nodded along.

'Why don't you show us, lover boy? Maybe we can give you moral support,' Mohit said.

'Yes, why don't you?' Ajay said.

'Maybe we'll be able to help you out. You can go and finally talk to her,' Abid said.

'No thanks! You buggers stay away from her,' Tubby said, gesturing with his arms, at which the boys snickered.

'I can see dead people,' Ajay said, doing a poor impression of Tubby with a laugh. 'Maybe it's some ghost chick only Tubby can see and communicate with.'

'Shut up, guys! All you think of is jokes. Abid aside, neither of you has gone out with a girl. And Mohit, hanging out with your younger sister and her friends doesn't count.'

Mohit looked annoyed and shook his head, when Abid stepped in.

'Why don't I go with him? I'm seeing Naina anyway and Tubby trusts me. I'll check her out and maybe even help Tubby speak to her,' Abid said, slapping Tubby's back.

'Swell,' Mohit said, rubbing his hands.

'Done deal,' Ajay said.

'Where do you see this girl anyway?' Abid asked. 'Is this outside Archies? Or did you see her on the side, outside Rhythms?'

Tubby nodded. 'Bugger, it's just round the corner after Mohit's apartment, straight past Richie's, and then down the road, next to

Kebab Korner, just outside Ice n Spice, two buildings before my Dad's office.'

'Down the road, just outside apna Ice n Spice?' Ajay asked.

'Yeah, just outside. She goes home in a van. I see her if I leave between three-thirty and four in the evening. After that, she's gone,' Tubby said, explaining fast, eating up half his words and moving from one foot to the other while swinging his arms.

'Good, so I'll come with you,' Abid said, before they saw Bouncer coming out of the classroom.

'Aye, all of you ples come with me to the Headmaster haan.'

'Sir ples, I mean please, one chance, sir,' Abid said.

'Give us another chance, sir,' Ajay said.

'I swear it wasn't us, sir. Someone from behind made the sounds,'

Mohit said. 'We really respect you, sir.'

'You know my older brother, sir, we don't do all this, sir,' Tubby said, gesticulating wildly.

'Aye no, Boman, ples I know you, but these other fellows, scoundrels, haan!' Bouncer looked threateningly from one boy to another.

'Please, sir,' they all said in unison. 'Sorry, sir.'

'Aye go to class ples,' he said, giving up. 'Next time I won't leave you haan,' he said, walking away like a bruised boxer.

◆

Later that evening, Abid and Tubby walked over to Ice n Spice, soon after school. They got there by 3:40 pm and stood outside the bakery, looking around discreetly.

'There she is,' Tubby said, tugging his arm. Abid noticed a tall, slim, brown-haired girl, with sharp features, hazel eyes and a tiny nose, looking like a dream, walk across the street towards the bakery. She wore an oversized sweater over her school uniform. She stood a few metres from them and removed her hair clip, letting her hair loose. She glanced in Tubby's direction and gave him a smile of recognition, while he stood gaping at her wide-eyed, thinking this was a bad idea.

'Go talk to her. She smiled at you,' Abid nudged him. He stood wonder-eyed, admiring her legs, for a moment wishing that he wasn't dating Naina.

'No, not now! It isn't the right time, it makes it obvious,' Tubby said. 'Let's go, now that you've seen she exists.'

'Well, come on, be a man! If I weren't dating Naina, she and I would be getting to know each other. I would be sitting inside Ice n Spice and feeding her mango mousse.'

'Don't do this, bugger...'

'Go on Tubby, say hello, be nice, be a man. I'm challenging you! Don't you have guts? I'll back you up.'

Tubby mustered courage, knowing that he wouldn't hear the end of it if he didn't, and walked over to her. 'Err...Hi. I'm Boman, from Shepherd's Boys...' he said softly, looking around self-consciously, extending his hand and then pulling it back.

'I'm Kanika, I've just moved from Shimla to Bangalore. My Dad, who's in the army, is posted here,' she said with a shy smile.

Just then Abid joined them. 'Hi, I'm Abid, glad to meet you,' he said.

'Hi,' she said cheerily. 'It's nice to meet you. I haven't made any new friends here. The girls are so stuck in their own cliques.'

'Don't worry; we're here now. We'll get you sorted. You can hang out with us. I'm Naina's boyfriend,' he said. 'Tub...Boman here is a star musician. He's the guitarist of our school band.' He slapped Tubby on his back, while Kanika smiled at him sweetly.

'I really like your bag, Boman,' she said, glowing with a smile.

Tubby took off his bag and showed it to her. It was a plain white Jansport bag with sketches of Mick Jagger, Steve Tyler, Santana strumming the guitar, The Undertaker and a Steve Austin 3:16 skull, drawn with a felt pen. The boys had also scrawled 'The Big Tub', 'Feed Me' and 'Burger Bawa' with permanent red and blue markers, which Kanika looked at with interest. Tubby smiled nervously.

'I really like Santana too,' she said, at which Tubby blushed.

'Why don't you have something to drink? It's quite warm today,' Abid said.

'I don't mind a Pepsi,' she said, still admiring the sketches.

'One Pepsi for me too,' Abid said, gesturing to Tubby, who walked off immediately to the bakery. He was back in a minute with two Pepsis and a Fanta for himself as well as a packet of chips, a double lamb burger and two samosas.

'I'm really hungry,' he said, at which Abid gave Kanika a knowing smile and took their bottles from him.

◆

The next day, all Abid spoke about with the boys was Kanika and about how they had hit it off with her.

'She even gave Tubby her phone number,' Abid said, giving Tubby a wink. 'Tubby's the rock star man. She's probably the hottest babe to set foot in Shepherd's—and remember, there have been three Miss Indias and one Miss World from across the street.'

'You're kidding! Dog's luck, huh, Tubby?' Ajay said, while Mohit gazed at him with envy. 'This sucks! Tubby and a hot babe? She probably finds him amusing.'

Tubby, who had been quiet and reticent all day, lost in his dreams of Kanika-land, turned around, looking irritated. 'Yes, and

I'm sure she doesn't like guys who watch porn all the time.'

'Really? How would you know, giant panda?' Mohit asked with a grimace.

'Because I spoke to her; I know what she's like. I'm not a zombie, like you. Go play Zelda on your computer.'

Ajay and Abid looked at each other and smiled as the insults were exchanged. Tubby and Mohit were going at each other again.

'Guys, chill, it's time for Bouncer's class. He's here already,' Ajay said.

◆

Later in the evening Tubby, crossing the street with his now-famous bag, saw Mohit, Abid and Ajay chatting animatedly with Kanika in Ice n Spice. 'How Deep Is Your Love' by the Bee Gees was playing in the background. He went across to them with a lump in his throat. He didn't want the whole gang around her.

'Come, come, I was just telling Kanika how you imitated good old Bouncer and our friend Mohit got kicked out,' Ajay said, as Kanika smiled. Mohit smiled sheepishly in the background, chomping on French fries.

'I didn't know you could imitate people so well, Tubby,' she said, with her sweetest smile and with laughter in her hazel eyes.

Tubby! Tubby thought, feeling annoyed. He looked at Abid with irritation.

'Yes, he can do the moonwalk too,' Mohit said, with his toothy grin, at which they all laughed.

'I have to go, my Dad is waiting,' Tubby said tersely, picking up his bag and lumbering out of the cafe, his cheeks flushed with anger and tears welling up in his eyes.

The rest of the group went quiet. 'Boman, I...' Kanika called out, at which he hesitated but didn't respond.

Abid came after him, matching his pace and catching up with him outside Richie Rich. 'Tubs, what happened?'

'Why did you have to bring those buggers to talk to her? I really like her man, and you guys are ridiculing me.' Abid saw a flash of anger in Tubby's eyes.

'Man, I'm sorry. I was standing with her and these guys came over. I couldn't not introduce them, what could I have said?'

'You didn't have to make fun of me in front of her,' Tubby said, sounding upset. He saw the three of them come out of Ice n Spice and walk with her to her van. He could see Ajay lean in and make conversation as a wide-eyed Mohit flashed his Dracula smile.

'I didn't tell them anything. These guys started asking "Where's Tubby," etc. She asked who this Tubby was. I said Tubby was your nickname. Then they started off with these stories of what happens in class. Anyway, you just come with me man. Don't ruin it. You like this girl.'

Tubby stopped for a moment, looking beyond Abid's shoulder. He noticed her gazing at Ajay intently and blushing, as he leaned close to her and flirted with her.

'Leave me alone, man,' he said, pushing Abid aside and walking away.

'What's with him?' Sunaina asked with a look of surprise. He had walked past her without a word, while she walked towards Abid.

'No, nothing, it's just that these guys went and made fun of him in front of the new girl. Let me get you something to eat, Naina,' Abid said, watching Tubby walk into the building where his Dad worked.

'Yes, I'm so hungry, let's go.'

♦

Eleven years later…

Boman was about to sneak out from a boring party a newspaper editor was hosting.

'Hi Boman, do you remember me?' a voice said from behind him.

Boman turned around. She looked familiar, a stunningly beautiful woman, smiling at him. She wore a stylish blue dress and diamond earrings. He felt himself go weak in the knees. It was as if time had stopped. He remembered those hazel eyes. 'Kanika…' he said, looking at her with awe and surprise. *She's still smashing,* he told himself.

'Said I Loved You But I Lied' faded away and 'Sealed With a Kiss' came on over the speakers, as a few couples who seemed like they were in their forties moved with their partners to the dance floor.

'You look the same, Boman,' she said.

'Not really, I've put on a few kilos and have lost some hair over the years,' he guffawed, pointing to his now-receding hairline with a smile.

'Ha ha, I didn't notice. Where have you been? I haven't seen you since my first few days in school. I do follow your blog, *Being Baltiwala*. I really like it. It's funny, especially your illustrations. I wanted to write to you, but didn't know what to say,' she said with a pout.

'Yes, it's been a long time. How have you been? What do you do?' He thought about her all the time. He had a picture of her in his head. He had written a song dedicated to her, a soulful ballad called 'Not Down That Road Again'.

'I've finished a fashion designing course. I'm opening a new boutique. Here's my card. Where are you at the moment?'

'Well, here and there. I'm a free bird. I contribute to newspapers and magazines. You must have seen my comic strips. I do a couple—*Boman's World* and *The Adventures of Dracula*. I'm writing a children's book and a graphic novel.'

She gazed at him with amazement. This calm and self-assured man was nothing like the fast-talking, self-conscious, acne-faced teenager she remembered.

'Wow! Living the dream, huh? Do you still play the guitar?'

'Yeah, all the time. I'm a part of a band—*Creatures of Sound*. I compose music; our band also does campus gigs. We've done gigs at Hard Rock. We play at Olio this weekend. You should come.'

'Wow, I didn't know that. I'll definitely be there. Where do I get tickets?'

'I have your card; maybe we can go there together. Come with me, you won't need a ticket,' he smiled. 'Maybe we'll play something by Santana as well.'

'Okay, ha, ha, sure. Call me; we'll work it out. I'd love to go,' she said, emptying her glass of wine.

'How's Ajay?' he asked. He noticed that she was at the party alone and had no rings on her fingers.

'I have no clue. We broke up a year after he went to Berkeley,' she said. 'I hear he's in New York. I have him on Facebook, but we don't really chat. He's married, I think.'

'Okay... I didn't know that. Too bad it didn't work out for you guys.'

'It's okay. It was eight years ago. A lot has happened since then; a few more break-ups were added to the collection,' she smiled, looking a little jaded. 'How's Abid? I haven't seen him and Sunaina since Ajay and I split up.'

'Naina and Abid got married two years ago,' he said.

'Wow, they really have lasting power, don't they?'

'Not really, they both separated last month; their marriage

didn't work. He has moved to Bombay now,' he said, sipping his beer.

'That's sad. They are nice people, both of them. Do you have Naina's number? I'll call her.'

'Sure, here it is,' he said, showing her the number on his iPhone.

'Where's the other guy? Mohit or Mohan was his name, right? Ajay and I hung out with Abid and Naina most of the time. I didn't see much of him.'

'No clue, I haven't seen him since school. Abid's the only one from school who I'm in touch with,' he said.

'Okay, it was really good seeing you after so long. I've got to go, but I'll see you at your gig this weekend, yeah?'

'Yes, I'll call you. And I'll come around and pick you up.'

'Great, I'll wait to hear from you soon. Good night then.' She leaned across and kissed him on his cheek before walking away with a smile and a wave.

Boman stood there dumbfound till Sriram slapped his back.

'She's a babe, machha,' he said.

'Hmm…' Boman said, walking to the bar to get another drink. He took out his wallet and removed a frayed and crumpled piece of paper. It was her phone number, one that she had scrawled twelve years back. A number he had never called because of what had happened all those years ago.

She was his first crush, a girl who broke his heart and changed everything around him. Mohit was the recipient of a swollen lip and a black eye in class the following day. Nobody called him Tubby after seeing him thrash Mohit. Boman stopped hanging out with the group and only reconciled with Abid and Naina after meeting them at one of his gigs, five years back.

Strange are the ways of the world, he thought. He looked at Kanika's new number on his handset, a number he was certainly going to call. He walked over to Sriram with his mug of beer and a big grin. *I Don't Want To Miss A Thing* by Aerosmith echoed over the speakers. His phone beeped, it was Kanika. 'Wanna catch-up for lunch at Ice n Spice tomorrow?' the message said.

Rishi and Me: A Love Story

IRA TRIVEDI

Rishi and Riya, Riya and Rishi. That was us, wasn't it? What happened to us, Rishi? One small mistake and this is what you do to me? Please Rishi, come back. Please. Rishi, I can't live without you. You promised me that we would be together forever, but where are we now? Please come back to me. I'm sorry. You know I didn't mean it, you know that.

Yours,
Riya

What struck me were his eyes. They were keenly intelligent yet aloof and full of hauteur. They were like sharp little daggers. When he looked at me, he got underneath my skin and knew everything that I was thinking. Not everything, but almost.

I walked into school, the new girl with the too-short skirt, the too-short socks, the too-tight shirt. The girl from 'Dilli' they used to say, hissing at me when I walked past. I was shy, unnerved and embarrassed, having been in an all-girls school all my life. Rishi was the gang-leader. He would throw chalk at me, tease me and pull my hair so hard that it brought tears to my eyes. When Mrs Agarwal, the history teacher, made us partners, sitting on the same bench, my life was hell. I stuck it out because I didn't want to be the loser girl who cried when she was teased. Rishi and his troops destroyed me, and I had never been as miserable as I was that year, and I cursed my parents for sending me to boarding school in the hellhole of Indore.

Dear Rishi,

You probably won't read this, like you haven't read the other letters I have written to you, but I have to keep on writing because I love you, and I know what I have done is despicable and I can't expect you to forgive me, but I have to try. Why? Because I love you. I know that you have a girlfriend, and that you are really happy in college, and of course you have managed to become the king of campus, like you have always been. But you have to forgive me, Rishi. You have to, because I won't be able to forgive me till you forgive me.

Yours unconditionally,
Riya

We were in the 11th standard, depressed and disgruntled—suffering from Post-traumatic stress from the horrid board exams we had taken last year. We were languorous, lazy seniors. At least I was. Next year, the 12th grade would bring responsibility, and then college and real life and all of that, but this year, I would just languish in my laziness and I would be fine. I had worked really hard over the past two years and had ranked 3rd in the 10th grade board exams. I was basketball champion, debate team champion, swimming captain, and had several lesser captainships tucked firmly under my belt. I had proved to myself that I could do it. With the ensuing ennui, boycott of academia and raging teenage hormones, my focus shifted to a dangerous and precarious but inevitable territory—boys.

And just like that, Rishi and I started dating. We had known each other since the 8th standard, been arch rivals in the 9th standard, best friends in the 10th standard, and now lovers in the 11th. Though the word 'lovers' is a bit of an exaggeration. All Rishi and I ever did was go into empty classrooms after school and sit across from each other, looking at each other with shy, lustful eyes. Sometimes we even held hands, but that was reserved for special occasions like birthdays. There were a few nervous intimate moments, like the time he plaited my hair for me in the squash courts. There was another time that he helped hook my bra, but there were two layers between my bra and his fingers—the shirt and the slip. We were in love, or at least he was, and I knew it. I guess girls know when boys are in love with them; we feel it in our bones.

At that time, I didn't realize what he meant to me, because that was my nature—careless, flighty and irresponsible. It's not like I hadn't warned him. I had. I told him that I was the most selfish creature he would ever meet. But he just smiled at me with those kind, laughing eyes, kissed my hand and told me that was just me, and that was why me loved me. I don't know why he fell in love with me, I don't know why anyone would, least of all someone as wonderful as Rishi. Why would he fall for someone as rotten as me? So there we were, Rishi and Riya, Riya and Rishi. Two lovers basking in our glorious bubbles of success, in our make-believe world. Him in love with me, and I in love with myself.

Dear Rishi,

I know we had some bad times, but don't you remember all the good times? Remember what fun we had in the 11th standard? Bunking all those classes, failing all those exams and then laughing about it. Winning all those basketball matches? You cheering for me, me cheering for you? Remember how they looked at us, our juniors? In awe and wonder. Remember the

*day of our coronation, as head-boy and head-girl, and the sweet
kiss that we shared after? Oh Rishi! That was the sweetest kiss
I will ever know. Rishi and Riya, Riya and Rishi. We were
lyrical, passionate, colloquial, abstruse, rigorous, humorous,
romantic, complex and playful, all at the same time. Rishi,
how could you not remember?*

Yours endlessly,
Riya

Abdul Salim Khan. Head-boy, hockey-captain, arsehole par
excellence. He was my ambrosia and an enigma. I saw him for the
first time on the hockey field, his carnal and loping grace transfixing
me on the spot as cheers for him bellowed on all sides. There was
something about him that had me pretty badly. I guess when a girl
has a crush on the guy, he knows it. I'm not sure how he knew,
I swear I hadn't told anyone, but he just did. I was in the 10th
standard, and Abdul started sending me notes, courtesy submissive
juniors, many via the hands of his most trusted junior and my
best friend—Rishi. It is only now that I realize how hard it must
have been for Rishi to hand over those devious, carelessly scrawled
parchments of paper (which, at that point, I stupidly thought were
as precious as love letters). The messages were most often of this
nature: 'You're hot', 'You've got a killer body and a killer shot', and
other such creative, highly thought-out scribbles that would make
me swoon with passion. What could Rishi possibly do? After all,
Abdul was his senior, his house-captain, head-boy and basketball
vice-captain. It couldn't have been a more lethal combination. He
simmered inside and never discussed the notes with me. I often
wondered if he even read them. He must have, how could he not?
If there was one guy capable of not reading the notes, it would have
been the sinfully faithful, horribly loyal love of my insignificant

life—Rishi. How could he not have noticed how I eagerly grabbed the notes from him, how I bit my lower lip trying to disguise the painful, coy smile that my lips would twist into, as if they had a mind of their own. He must have noticed, but he never said a word, to me or to anyone else. Normally, he would have teased me till I was blue, and I him, but this time somehow, it was different.

One day it came, and even if Rishi knew what the note said, he didn't behave any differently than he ever did. He handed me the note in Mr Sule's math class as all talk of geometry drifted gracefully over my head. All I could think about was chemistry, and maybe even a little bit of biology. This carelessly torn parchment of paper said:

Meet me. After games. Art Block—ASK

A little shiver went up my spine. Art block. Everyone knew what happened there or, as measly 10th graders, we heard of what happened there.

It was the first time that I was meeting him, close-up that is.

For the past two years, I had imbibed him with my eyes at hockey matches and basketball matches, making sure I got a seat at lunch time that would give me a bird's eye view of my beloved. I was so nervous. What would I do? Shake his hand? Give him a hug? What would I even say to him? He was the head-boy, hockey-captain, big man around campus, and I, just an inconsequential 10th grader. A reticent and boring girl with her head buried in her books.

Somehow, I don't even know why, we hit it off. At least I thought we did. We began meeting every day, after games at the Art Block, bunking classes together, and then he began sneaking me into his dorm room. In retrospect, I am not sure what I saw in him. And everyone had warned me that ASK was a born arsehole, that he had had affairs aplenty, with girls of all ages, shapes and sizes, often leaving them heartbroken, treating them like shit. No one had anything nice to say about him, but would I listen to them? Obviously not. They were all horribly jealous. Here I was, a measly 10th grader, dating the big man on campus.

Rishi and I drifted apart. I didn't realize it was because of Abdul, probably because I was too obsessed with myself to ever realize it.

It ended as quickly as it had started. One day, he just stopped showing up. I went to the Art Block every day and he didn't come. I called him in his dorm, he didn't pick up. He appeared completely normal, feigned amnesia when he saw me, when what had seemed like just moments ago we had been locked in each other's arms. I wanted to run to him, grab him and ask what was wrong, but I couldn't possibly do that without drawing attention to myself, especially from the teachers. There were always so many people around, hordes of people in blue and white spiralling around me, keeping him and me apart. I wrote note after note, sending them with Rishi, who just shrugged his shoulders and put them in his pocket. I begged him, I screamed at him. 'What did he say,' I asked, and he avoided my eyes and just shrugged. I accused Rishi of not delivering the notes, told him that he had torn us apart on purpose. Rishi just looked at me, pathetic in my sickness, sadness in his kind, piercing eyes.

After the frenzy came the quiet depression that snuck onto me at the most inopportune times, leaving me paralyzed. No one knew what to do with me; my Headmistress thought it was the stress of the looming board exams, my friends were too distraught with their exams to care about my lovesickness. I failed one exam after the other. My teachers shook their head, asking me to 'shape up'. If I wanted to be house-captain, I would need the grades. I sunk deeper into a quagmire of unhappiness and longing. At the end, when I was on the brink of doom, it was Rishi who rescued me. It was Rishi who force-fed me mathematical formulae, chemical conundrums and the Indian Constitution. It was he who made sure that I studied and that I ate three meals a day. It was Rishi who held me while I cried, it was Rishi who made sure I survived.

Dear Rishi,

Annual Day is in two weeks. Will you come? Please? I know that this day is painful for you. It is for me too, but I love you, Rishi, and I want to see you again. Even if it is just hi-bye types, it would be lovely to just see you again. Rishi, everyone will be there, our entire batch, all our old friends, don't you want to come? I know you have a girlfriend now, I know you have moved on, but I have to see you Rishi. Please come. Please.

Yours always,
Riya

Twelfth standard, senior year. Rishi and Riya, Riya and Rishi. He was head-boy and I head-girl. We were the prince and princess of campus. We were happy and fulfilled like we had never been before, basking in our glory and our love for each other. Could life get any better than this, I wondered. I guess happiness never lasts. This kind of bliss was fickle and inconstant.

Abdul came back for the annual day, dressed in a black band-gala with a red scarf around his strong neck. He looked so handsome that I thought I would faint. Shivers of desire went up my spine and I remembered those stolen moments in the Art Block, those fleeting instances in his dorm room. A cold, macabre wind blew over my dead heart bringing messages of longing and unfulfilled desire.

Behind the tent, he handed me the bottle. I took a swig and gulped, holding my breath so I wouldn't have to taste it. My first kiss, my first drink, all with Abdul. He took the bottle from my hand, drank out of it and then handed it back to me. I took another and then another and, before I knew it, I was walking hand in hand with him to the Art Block. Him, glorious and regal, and me, plain and inconsequential. The gallant colours of head-girl now seeming disturbingly drab.

We walked into the darkness and, suddenly, despite the drowsy, soporific effects of the vile liquid, I felt something dour, dark and disturbing, and I knew what I was about to do was frightfully wrong. My brain was like a black, impregnable dome, and no amount of rational arguments could slip into it. I wanted to scream, to turn around and run away from him, but I couldn't. I stood there like a robot while he pinned me down, unbuttoning my shirt, sliding his cold hands, hard as rocks from years of wielding hockey sticks, through the starch of my shirt, through the thin muslin of my slip, underneath the rough cotton of my bra, touching my warm breast, squeezing it till I quietly yelped in pain. He undid the hook of my heavy, pleated skirt and it fell noiselessly in a bundle around my ankles. He put his cold hand on the small of my back and his mouth on mine.

Suddenly I heard the susurrus of surprise, which was neither from him nor from me. Then the pattering of swift feet running away. A rhythm which I, though tone-deaf, could recognize in the dead of my sleep. A rhythm that was a perfect pearl in its roundness and plenitude. The rhythm of Rishi's graceful gait rang inside my drunken head as I untangled myself from Abdul.

Just like that, it was over. Rishi and Riya, Riya and Rishi. Our blossoming romance cruelly nipped in the bud because of my stupidity. He never spoke to me after that. I saw him deteriorating, slipping steadily down the same slope that I had two years ago, except there was no one to rescue him. He wouldn't let me close to him. He kept me far away as I watched his downhill progress. Rishi failed two of his board exams, but was able to spend the summer studying for them, and finally passed. His basketball got him into a mediocre college. Not only had I shattered his heart into tiny, sharp pieces, I had cruelly destroyed his future as well. I did well, well enough to make it back to Delhi, my original home, far away from those aching memories of boarding school in Indore. It was only when I was away that I began to realize how much I missed him, and how dearly I had loved him.

Dear Rishi,

You didn't come. I thought you would surprise us, surprise me. But you didn't come. Why? I asked Akshay how you were, and he said you were really good. You're the basketball captain, aren't you? A fresher becoming the basketball captain is really, really amazing. But Rishi, why didn't you come? You know, none of the boys would talk to me, they didn't even look at me. They all blame me for you not coming. They blame me for everything—for the exams that you failed, for the shots that you missed, for the time they had to take you to the hospital because you had slit your wrists. Is it fair to blame everything on me? Come on Rishi, write to me? I love you, you know that. I miss you, and I worry now because I'm not sure when I'll see you again.

Yours forever,
Riya

Knockout

AHMED FAIYAZ

'I can't believe this! We are in real trouble now,' Achal said as he rushed into the classroom with a look of horror on his face.

'What can't you believe, moon-face?' Siddharth said, while Rajiv and Abrar stood around, looking bored. The four of them sat on the same bench in the last row and were known to be the brat pack of IX B.

'Sid, have you heard?'

'Heard what?' Siddharth was the leader of the group and the mastermind behind a number of pranks the Brat Pack had played on the teachers.

'Mrs Sampat has gone on maternity leave...'

'You realized that now?' Rajiv asked with a mischievous grin.

'Yes, wasn't it a *bit* obvious!' Abrar guffawed.

'Bro, I know. But do you know who has come in as a replacement?' The school was finding it hard to get a replacement for Mrs Sampat. None of the current crop of teachers wanted her classes allocated to them. A couple of them had threatened to resign if they were given any more sessions with IX B.

'Who? Don't tell me it's your Dad?' Achal shook his head in response.

'Is it your Mum, then?' Rajiv asked.

'No guys!' Achal rubbished the idea. 'Imagine my parents teaching us physics. It's Pagal Pinto from St. Xavier's!'

'Hell! I've heard about this guy. I hear he chased some kid around the cricket field with a bat to bash him up,' Abrar chipped in with a mixture of relish and trepidation.

'Yes, he got thrown out of Xavier's last year for banging some fellow's head against the blackboard. The chap's parents threatened to call the news channels, and the school agreed to make Pinto retire at the end of the year. He taught there for twenty-five years,' Achal said. 'Even my uncle remembers getting hammered by him. My cousin got lucky because he is just in the eighth…'

'Hmm… And now he is here, is it? Don't worry, corporal punishment isn't allowed in our school,' a chubby faced Rajiv declared before taking another bite from his samosa.

'Let him come! We'll deal with him much like we dealt with Compass and Foggy,' Sid said with a mock punch at Rajiv's tummy and smirked. Compass was their mathematics teacher, and Foggy was the geography teacher who made every attempt to miss his allotted period at IX B. He often offered his class to others in the staffroom who had unfinished portions to make up for. The teachers dreaded coming to the classroom that was known to hold the most notorious gang in school. Compass had fainted the week before when he'd walked in to see a dead snake, stolen by the boys from the biology lab, on the floor by the entrance.

Achal still looked worried and shook his head. 'Bro, it isn't going to be easy, I tell you. He used to be a boxer in the old days. He's a very frustrated guy. The story goes that he became a teacher since he was in love with a young primary school teacher at Xavier's. Then she went and became a nun and his life went to hell. He's been bashing everything that walks since then.'

'I hear he comes drunk to the classroom, and even slips out now and then for a shot of his favourite whisky,' Abrar said.

'Sounds like a fun guy, let him come,' Rajiv said before he bit into another samosa.

'Yes, he'll know better than to mess with us. Pyarelal or Foggy must've briefed him already,' Sid added as he dribbled the basketball on the floor of the classroom. Pyarelal was the Hindi professor who, after 6 months, was still to finish the first chapter of the textbook. A failed actor, he often narrated lines from films and told them stories the film sets, reliving the days when he had played sidekick to Dharmendra. The boys cheered on his performance, happy as long as Katha Sarovar was not on the agenda!

♦

The classroom went silent suddenly. A grey-haired man of medium height walked through the door with a briefcase in hand. He had a thick moustache and was well-built, with strong arms. He was unlike their roly-poly, half-bald professors, such as Pyarelal and Compass, who couldn't run from one end of the classroom to another without getting a heart attack. A good-looking man, he was an impressive sight with his thin-rimmed glasses, the mole on his cheek, and his expensive tie. He looked quite like an Indian version of Robert de Niro with a moustache and glasses.

'Stand up all of you. Quite a bunch of imps I've heard,' he said as he scanned the room and walked down the passage between the two rows on either side of the classroom.

'Good morning, sir,' the boys said in chorus. It wasn't something they were used to, as Foggy and Compass often crept in and crept out of the classroom.

'Hmmrff ! Not such a nice morning seeing me here, is it? You fellows have been having a gala time for the past month. Take out your textbooks. Today we will learn about speed and velocity. We'll also do some sums,' he said in his gruff baritone. His voice, which usually commanded respect and instilled fear in the hearts of students, rang through this new batch.

'Hey Rajiv, come on…make some noise,' Sid said nudging him in his belly.

'Not now, maybe later,' Rajiv said while staring at what was being written on the blackboard.

'Sid, bro, watch out man. I'm telling you, don't mess with him,' Achal said.

'Shut up guys, he's staring at us,' Abrar muttered while smiling at Mr Pinto, who returned the smile with a grimace.

'Here, you fools in the last row, am I not loud enough back there? Take out your bloody textbook man, page 72. Now!'

'Wow, son of a gun!' Sid whispered to Rajiv and Achal who sat on either side.

'I thought I thaw a putty cat,' Rajiv chirped out in the voice of Tweety, the cartoon character, while Mr Pinto had his back turned to the blackboard.

He turned around. There was pin drop silence. 'Don't get funny with me, I warn you!' he hollered, banging his fist on a table in the front row. Rahul, a short kid with larger than normal ears, snickered in the 2nd row. Mr Pinto was upon him in a flash. He grabbed his shirt and lifted him up by his collar.

'The next time you show your teeth in my class, I'll box you,' he barked, raising his fist and keeping it at kissing distance from Rahul's nose. He dropped him suddenly and walked back to the blackboard trying to regain his composure. He muttered something under his breath that sounded like 'cowards' and 'scoundrels'.

Sid and gang began humming in the last row and the rest of the class immediately caught on. The humming sound grew increasingly loud. Pinto swung around again and the noise stopped. 'Here, this noise…it irritates me!' He walked over to Rahul again and lifted him up by his collar.

'Tell me I say, you little monkey, who is it?' he said, leaning in threateningly with a manic look in his eyes.

'Not I sir, please sir, it wasn't me. It came from behind, sir!' he pointed to the back of the class.

Pinto dropped him and paced around the room. 'All you good for nothing loafers who come to school, why I say? Do you come here for an education? Does anyone here want to learn? Ask your parents to send you to the zoo. Bloody fools!'

He went back to the blackboard. 'Copy down this diagram,' he said, as he turned around to draw with precision on the blackboard.

'Errr, what's up doc?' Rajiv screeched, this time in the voice of Bugs Bunny.

'Here, who the hell is it? If you have the guts stand up to me, I say! I'll bash you up, you little fellow,' he said pointing at the elf-like Rahul who was howling with laughter. The whole class was in splits. He rushed towards Rahul when Rajiv stood up.

'Sir, I'm the one who made the noise. And you can't raise your hand against me. It's against the rules,' Rajiv said with a straight face as the classroom went quiet and everyone turned around to stare at him.

'I will knock your teeth out, boy,' Mr Pinto screamed as he charged towards him and swung his fist at Rajiv's cheek. The enraged teacher struck him again with a left jab before Rajiv covered his face with both hands, groaning in pain. 'Can't do anything, eh? Put your hand down, I say,' Pinto said before slapping his other cheek, the sound of which vibrated through the classroom. The students looked at him shell-shocked. It was the first time they had seen the mighty Rajiv Lalvani being roughed up like the sidekick of a villain in a Hindi film. He pulled Rajiv out of the last row and, dragging him by his ear, pushed him out of the classroom before shutting the door behind him.

By the end of the period, Mr Pinto had earned the fear and respect of most of the students present in the class. He shut his briefcase and quietly walked out with a calm look on his face like he had been on an evening stroll along the Bandstand promenade.

Sid walked to the front of the class and asked everyone to remain seated. 'It's time for war,' he declared.

◆

The next day, Mr Pinto walked in wearing a striped shirt and an impressive new tie. He had confidence in his gait and a relaxed expression on his face. *These bloody idiots should know what I'm capable of,* he told himself as he opened his briefcase and took out his papers. The class stood up with rapt attention to wish him loudly.

'Good morning, sir,' they said before he gestured for them to take their seats.

He could hear the faint sound of music in the background. He caught the words, *'Living next door to Alice...'*

'Here, put off the damn music, man. I'll bash you up if I find you,' he said with a stony face. His cheeks had turned crimson red. The music grew louder. *'Alice? Who the fuck is Alice?'* And the sound of drumbeats was clearly audible.

'What the hell?' He walked down from the elevated platform towards the back row and stopped in his tracks. He couldn't move beyond the 4th row as his path was blocked by school bags and lunch bags.

'Here, whose bags are these? Get them out of my way, you rascals.' Everyone kept a straight face and looked intently into their textbooks. Pinto turned his gaze to fix it on his favourite punching bag, little Rahul.

'Sir, not mine, sir. My bag is here,' he squeaked, pointing at a bag twice his size. He had refused to play any part in the fun and games.

He looked at his other target, Rajiv, who wasn't in the last row but sitting quietly in the first row with a straight face. 'Not mine either, sir. Some of our seniors keep their bags here.' Now the music changed to 'Macarena' and the classroom erupted with laughter. 'It's coming from outside, sir,' Rahul pointed out of the window at the back of the classroom.

'What nonsense!' Pinto grunted before stamping his way through the bags as he moved ahead. He felt something stir and stepped back.

The dog was awake now and growled at him. He had stepped on Sunshine, a stray mutt that the school watchman and peons had adopted. Sunshine had fallen asleep after being fed well by the boys and had been covered by one of the bags.

'Good dog, now step back,' Mr Pinto said before taking a step back himself. 'Someone get him out of the way. Shoo, shoo, go away.' The boys were in splits as Sunshine leapt over the bags and ran towards Mr Pinto before knocking him over and scampering out of the classroom.

A hapless Mr Pinto, whose glasses had fallen off, stood up with the assistance of Rahul. 'He's not known to bite, sir,' the big-framed Rajiv turned around and said amiably from the first row as the boys snickered and laughter reverberated through the classroom.

'Here, enough now, you scoundrels!' Pinto dusted off his tie and wiped the sweat on his brow with the palm of his hand.

He turned around and walked to his briefcase. 'Open your damn books you good-for-nothing fellows.' He opened his briefcase and jumped with a start. 'Oh my God!' Laughter again. A toad jumped out of the briefcase and hopped out of the classroom. He looked around the classroom with an expression of shock and disbelief. 'You are here to learn. Have some respect for the Master,' he said, with his face turning deep red as he shook his fist. In the other hand, he waved what he thought were his papers. 'I am here to give you an education, you fools.'

'Of course, we can't wait,' came a snide remark from the last row. It was Sid.

'Where can I order a copy of your textbook, sir?' Achal asked from behind.

The boys continued to laugh at him. Some pointed and snorted at the adult magazine he was holding up in his right hand. 'What the…? Where are my papers?'

'Can I borrow it for a while, sir?' Abrar shouted from the last row.

He put the magazine back in the briefcase and turning his gaze away from the boys who were pointing and snickering at him, he stormed out of the classroom.

Thunderous applause ran through the classroom. There was the slapping of backs and the banging of fists on tables. The boys sang *We Will Rock You* and stomped on the floor as Rajiv strummed a mock guitar before his hooting audience. Rajiv and Achal came to the front of the class to re-enact what had gone down a few moments ago. 'Bloody hell, here I will box you,' Rajiv imitated Mr Pinto's favourite catchphrase as the classroom rang with applause and celebration.

'I don't think he'll have the guts to show up for tomorrow's class,' Sid said.

'Haan, we put him through an experience he won't forget,' Abrar added.

'I told my cousin and he was stunned by our plan. He says that Pinto will go on a bender and come to class filled with rage and beat up a few more people,' Achal said.

The next morning, Mr Pinto paced down the hallway a couple of times before decisively striding into the classroom. Sunshine slept by the door as Mr Pinto entered and walked quietly towards his desk. He ignored the snorts and smirks, set down his briefcase and pulled out the *Playboy*. The whole class stared at it and there was a murmur in the last row.

'It's *Playboy* time,' Sid shouted out.

'Now, now boys. Let's not discuss yesterday's textbook, shall we? You can keep that discussion for your biology class,' he beamed as laughter filled the air. 'Now why don't you boys settle down? I want each of you to introduce yourselves and to tell me what you like about physics. Let's make this fun,' he said, walking down the aisle and breaking into a calm smile.

'You can come after class and take back your magazine,' he said leaning in and speaking softly to Rajiv within earshot of Sid and the others.

'And you're Siddharth, right?' Sid nodded. 'Hmm… Any plans to sing and dance about Alice today? You're quite the crooner aren't you?'

'No, sir,' Sid replied sheepishly as Pinto gazed piercingly at him while his face bore a warm smile.

'Good, there shouldn't be. Else I'll make you stand on stage and sing for the whole school,' he said softly. Sid nodded and turned his gaze to the floor. 'Take out your book and move to the first bench. Now!' He was all the more intimidating because of the softness of his voice.

He turned his gaze to Achal and grinned at him. 'And you, egghead, you have a very familiar face, man. Was your brother my student?' he asked with an air of authority.

'No sir, yes sir. My uncle, sir,' Achal said. He fumbled with his pen and dropped it to the floor and, in his nervousness, nudged Rajiv in his tummy as he bent to pick it up. Rajiv held his tummy and groaned while everyone laughed.

'Funny guy, egghead! Your uncle looks strikingly similar, he remembers me, doesn't he?'

'Y-y-yes, sir.'

'Good, alright then,' he said with his intimidating smile. 'Anyone I've boxed remembers me. And Rajiv, you may not want to keep your sick leave note in the folds of an interesting magazine. Here you go.' He handed back a folded note and turned to walk to the front of the class.

Relax, he told himself as Rajiv smiled back at him with respect.

Sororicide

PARITOSH UTTAM

The moment she walked into the classroom, it was clear to everyone that she was hopelessly out of place. It was as good as pinning a white sheet on her back with the letters printed in bold—I AM A MISFIT.

Sitting in his usual place on the last bench, beside Bulldog, Skipper shook his head, baffled. Someone, perhaps in the Selection Committee, had surely played a prank on her. Bulldog's jaw dropped. He nudged Skipper in the ribs and said, 'Don't tell me she's the one? The new teacher?'

Skipper did not reply. She had taken her place in front of the blackboard. A hope flickered in his mind that she would know how to deal with them. It was a long shot, but maybe she had the confidence to take them in hand.

What she wore, however, did not appear confidence-inspiring. There was nothing wrong with her plain salwar suit in a subdued blue shade, but it looked as if it were chosen so as not to make her stand out. Clearly, it wasn't a set that she had bought especially for this occasion, but it was equally apparent that it was well cared for.

She opened her mouth, met their blank stares, turned back to the blackboard and fumbled with the chalk. Hesitation clouded her petite, five-foot-two frame and snuffed out his hope. The chalk fell, broke. It screeched when she picked it up and wrote on the board.

When she faced them again, she had a painful smile. 'I am

Anita Thomas,' she said, thumbing back needlessly at the scrawl on the blackboard, which Skipper now deciphered as her name. Her voice shook as badly as her hand had while writing. 'It's my first day as a teacher,' she said with a ghastly chuckle.

Spare us the candour, please, Skipper thought and shut his eyes in agony. As if it took a Sherlock Holmes to discover it was her first ever attempt at teaching. She was only making it worse for herself. When he opened his eyes, he found Bulldog looking at him curiously.

'I told you my name. It's your turn now. Why don't you tell me your names? Let's get to know each other and be friends,' she said, breaking into a torturous laugh that came out as an embarrassing snort. This line, Skipper felt, must have been prepared and practised for a week. She was at a loss about what to do with her hands. She folded them in front, then held them behind and, finally, let them hang limply by her sides.

She couldn't have picked a worse opening. Everybody groaned. They hated these attempts to be interactive or to get them involved. The best bet would have been to leave them alone. Yet, they gave their names one by one, grudging and sullen, perhaps still in shock. How could the Selection Committee have foisted someone like her on them? It was as though a calf had strayed into the midst of a pride of lions. It wasn't fair game. Bulldog still looked baffled at her presence.

As Skipper's turn approached, he realised that the way he answered would set the tone for the future. It was always that way— the rest of the class emulated his indifference or rudeness to the teacher. When Mr Rastogi had come, the class had been moved by the old man's doddering gait, but Skipper was firm that they show no clemency towards him. It was the other way with Mr Pereira, whose know-all brashness antagonized the class immediately, but

Skipper was keen on giving him a chance. Later, however, he had changed his mind.

The point was that the rest followed his lead, as if they knew unanimously that what Skipper did would be correct. Not entirely unanimous, though. He always felt the tug of a little anti-current from Junior, but he would not dare to go against Skipper openly. So if Skipper decided to be nice to Miss Anita...

But why did he want to be nice to her? It must be the meekness in her eyes, that doe-like timidity, ready to take flight at anybody's approach, which carried over into her manner. It made him want to stand beside her, one impenetrable bulwark against all tribulations that could come her way, and tell her, 'Don't worry, I am here now.' He felt protective—that was it—she inspired protectiveness.

What if he stood and said, 'Look guys, can't you see this is different? We should not trouble Miss Anita at all. She is not like the others. Those young men who thought they were too smart to teach us, or the old ones who never bothered to... Heckling them, being rude to them was fine... They asked for it. But not Miss Anita.

'I mean, boys, take a look at her. It isn't fair. How can this five-foot-something chit of a girl handle the rowdiest class in the toughest school in the city? The Selection Committee must be crazy. Or maybe they warned her, but she was desperate for a job. Whatever, it isn't her fault. She's so scared she can't hold a chalk without dropping it.

'So guys, lay off her just this once, for my, for your Skipper's sake. Because your Skipper feels...that she reminds him of...of his sister. Which is strange, considering he never had a sister.'

He would sit quietly in the stunned silence that would follow. Then would come a deafening round of applause, amid which Miss Anita would look at him, eyes shining with gratitude.

Nice try. Howls and jeers would fill the room. Junior would

scream, 'Skipper has gone soft on the first teacher he sees in a skirt.' Or salwar. The details did not matter. It would amount to the same thing. This would be Junior's chance and he would not miss it. How could he protect Miss Anita and yet save himself from ridicule? He would fall from the pedestal the class had placed him on. Bulldog's dumb gaze of admiration would transfer to Junior. The mantle of Skipper would pass on to Junior.

Bulldog nudged him in the ribs again and Skipper realised Miss Anita was waiting for him to reveal his name.

'Skipper,' he said.

'Skipper? That's your name?' Miss Anita asked with a doubtful smile.

'Yeah. They call me Skipper. Not good enough for you?' he said brusquely and winced as her smile vanished. Her face turned red. No one had probably ever talked to her that way. She looked as if she had been slapped for some mistake she thought she had made. Something in Skipper's gaze had probably caught her eyes: some hint of kindness, of amiability…but his reply had shocked her. She became flustered and turned to Bulldog. He gave an ugly grin that creased the fat jowls which had given him his nickname.

'Bulldog!' he barked. Miss Anita gave a jump and the class burst out laughing. 'They call me Bulldog, what can I do?' Skipper felt like smashing his fist into Bulldog's thickset mouth.

But from that moment, Miss Anita's fate at the hands of the class was sealed. Replies to her grew ruder and more outrageous. They gave their nicknames, or coined new ones on the spot. Blockhead. Wadsworth. Longfellow. Genius. Junior. Skipper heard Junior's low growl and knew he was forestalled—he had had no option but to follow Skipper's lead.

Yet Miss Anita carried on, spurred by some misplaced zeal of duty and masochism, giving everyone a chance even when she knew the whole thing had become a farce.

Oh Miss Anita, Skipper's heart sang out mutely, surely you don't imagine you are going to win us all over with your niceness. Like that lesson in the textbook—*To Sir With Love. To Miss Anita With Love.* It doesn't happen that way. No, we are incorrigible, we are brutes. We don't deserve you.

It did not become any better as the period progressed. She grew rattled. The chalk fell two more times from her hand. There were four girls in the class of thirty and she looked at them. But they were always so steeped in the lassitude of indifference that Skipper knew it was futile for her to expect any sympathy from them. The four talked only among themselves and the boys had long given up bothering them.

Finally, the period ended. The relief on Miss Anita's face was palpable. Skipper was sure she would sob into her kerchief as soon as she reached the staffroom. Before leaving, she gave him an accusing glance that cut his heart. She held him responsible, it was clear. He had started it all, hadn't he? He was the Skipper, wasn't he, the captain of the ship leading his men?

He wanted to run out after her and declare, 'No, I am not like the others. Please don't think of me that way. They—Bulldog and Junior and the rest—forced me to do it. I have this reputation to maintain...I am supposed to be a tough guy. If I went soft on you, they would laugh at me. Junior would take over. You know Junior? That skinny guy in the corner? He's bad, he's really mean. Not like me. Please try to understand.'

The class dissolved in a paroxysm of laughter as soon as Miss Anita stepped out. Junior looked thoughtful and Bulldog sat strangely silent while the rest fell about their seats. Skipper knew she could hear the hoots of derision following her. He would have to make up. He could not let her think of him as a bully, the rowdy of the class. Maybe he could meet her and explain, but it would have to be somewhere outside, away from school and away from Junior's prying and Bulldog's bewildered eyes.

◆

The sun had set a long time back, the moon was still in its first quarter phase and the few streetlamps, not yet neon-ized, shed paltry circles of fluorescent light. The poor illumination suited Skipper as his silhouette came up the road leading to the staff and faculty quarters. He had found out at school that Miss Anita had taken up accommodation in this colony, but he did not know which one of the houses he was looking at belonged to her.

The unlit, apologetic looking one at the end of the row of houses could be where she lived, he thought. Somehow, the unassuming, retreating air of the house went hand-in-hand with Miss Anita. Maybe the accommodation was one of the reasons she took this job.

Did she live alone or with her family? Skipper imagined a doddering old mother, abandoned by her sons and now completely dependent on her daughter. Or the place where she lived with her family was so cramped that she had been compelled to break out and earn her own breathing space.

Skipper decided the best way would be to wait in the inky cover of a gulmohar tree at the side of the road, a few feet from the entrance to the colony. Something moved in the shadows beside him. He whirled around and saw the stout outline of another person.

'Skipper?' came the voice, doubtfully.

'Bulldog! What are you doing here?' Skipper exclaimed.

'I…I came…What about you?'

'I came to give Miss Anita a message, you know,' Skipper sniggered, sounding hollow to his own ears. But Bulldog was dumb, he wouldn't suspect him. What had he come here for though?

'You too? I have also come for that. We shall give it to her together now, eh Skipper?' Bulldog poked him in the ribs and laughed.

Skipper was thankful for the darkness that hid his expression. The ferocity of his anger surprised him. He had never loathed Bulldog more. In the limited visibility, with his thick face and bulbous eyes, he looked even more hideous. It was as if he groomed his ugliness the way others did their good looks.

'I think she lives there,' Bulldog said, pointing to the house in the corner. 'Let's wait. She might return soon.'

They heard somebody approaching and Skipper tensed. He moved forward but Bulldog held him back. It was somebody else.

Skipper's pulse was pounding so hard, it was a wonder Bulldog could not hear it. What would he do if Miss Anita came now? Could he confess to Bulldog? Maybe he would not mock, but he *would* be perplexed. And if he told Junior... He looked askance at Bulldog, trying to find a clue, the little encouragement he needed to reveal his secret. But under the canopy that hovered as opaque as a concrete ceiling, it was too dark to make out Bulldog's expression.

Five minutes later, they heard footfalls again. 'It's her!' Bulldog whispered fiercely in Skipper's ear. Indeed it was. Still in the same clothes she had worn in the morning, Miss Anita was trudging up the road, her gaze fixed on the ground. Her arms hung awkwardly at her sides, not swinging in tandem with her gait. It reminded him of the clumsiness of her hands in the morning. A pang pierced Skipper's heart.

They stepped out of the shadows just as she reached the tree. Miss Anita gasped in horror and jumped. Strong men would have quailed at the sight of Bulldog's sneering face popping out of the darkness.

'Good evening,' Skipper said.

'What do you want?' Her voice came out weakly.

'Didn't you recognize us? We are your students.'

'Oh.' Miss Anita squinted at them to place their features. Then she straightened. Bulldog's face was unmistakable. And she remembered Skipper. 'But what do you want?' She sounded braver after recognizing who they were.

'We just wanted to tell you something, since you are new to the school,' Skipper said. He hurried on, pre-empting her, 'It would be better if we said it outside school.'

Miss Anita waited, a little curiosity entering her expression.

'Some of the boys in our class have flunked once. They don't want to flunk again. Please see to it that they don't flunk in your subject.'

'Well, that's not in my hands. If they study, they will pass.'

'You don't understand.' Skipper glanced at Bulldog who stood silent and surly in the partial moonlight. Skipper knew he had no choice but to go ahead with it. His tone became menacing, 'The boys will not like it if they flunk again. Then they will become angry. And when they are angry they do bad things. So it would be in everyone's interest that you see to it that they do not flunk.'

'What is this? Are you threatening me?' She spoke bravely, but Skipper knew she was scared. He stood a head taller than her and Bulldog was twice her girth. He hated Bulldog for being there, he hated Junior and the whole class and the Selection Committee. And most of all, he hated himself.

'Not threatening, just advising.'

'I will report this to the Principal.'

'The boys would not like that either.'

Miss Anita looked at him with a mixture of fear and loathing. Her cheeks quivered and, for a moment, he thought she would burst into tears. She whirled around and, with rapid strides, walked away from them into the colony, without looking back.

Skipper and Bulldog watched her depart in silence and did not break it until she had disappeared inside the house in the corner. They waited but no lights came on.

Skipper said, 'So you think she got the message we came to give her?'

'Sure, Skipper,' Bulldog laughed. 'She got it all right. You were too good.'

'Think she will tell the Principal?'

'Nah. You scared her proper. She would not dare.'

'Hmm.' After a moment, Skipper said, 'She must hate us now, right?'

'Yeah,' Bulldog said, abruptly.

They did not speak again. They walked on, back down the poorly lit road, breathing the same cloud of shame and horror, each mourning the loss of a sister he never had.

Reason

AHMED FAIYAZ

Mr Wilcox walked into Richards Bakery in his evening suit. His cheeks were flushed from the three glasses of whisky he'd had before he left for the bakery. 'The usual loaf of bread eh, Swami,' he said in his English accent. The British had left but Mr Wilcox, the Principal of St. Martins High School, stayed on. After all, he was born in India, and so were his parents. The affable Englishman was popular in the local community and did his best to engage with them at a social level.

'Ah, Mr Iqbal. Good evening!' he beamed, with his puffed up chest.

'And a good evening to you too, sir,' Mr Iqbal said, holding on to the leash of his Pomeranian pup and staying a safe distance away from the drunk Englishman. Mr Iqbal was a respected businessman in the neighbourhood. He stood there looking regal in his white sherwani, a deep frown on his face.

'So, how are you feeling today, Mr Iqbal? I heard about your recent health problems…'

'I'm much better now, it was a minor stomach infection,' Mr Iqbal said with irritation. He turned to look at Swami. 'How long do I have to wait for the buns? It's suppertime and my wife and kids are waiting.'

Swami muttered that his parcel would be ready in five minutes.

'Anyway Mr Iqbal, my heartiest congratulations to you and

your family,' Mr Wilcox said, taking Mr Iqbal's hand and shaking it excitedly. 'It must be a good feeling, eh, new member of the family!'

'Yes…of course.' Mr Iqbal looked flabbergasted and stared at Swami, who stood with a blank expression on his face, for help.

'So is it a boy or a girl?'

These damn Englishmen, Mr Iqbal muttered to himself. 'It's a she.'

Mr Wilcox had a barmy look in his eyes and a wry grin. 'What is its name?' he asked, emphasizing 'it', and smirking in Swami's general direction.

'Rani,' Mr Iqbal said curtly, while the pup whimpered.

'Queen, eh? Strange name for a Muslim family.'

'What does religion have to do with it?'

'No, I'm just saying… I'm glad you have such progressive views for a man living in post-partition India, Mr Iqbal. Who does she resemble?'

'I'm not sure. Her mother, I guess. They all do, don't they?' He was waiting for this painful conversation to end.

'Of course they do, the little rascals. She must be crying a lot at night, must be keeping you awake well past your bedtime. It's a difficult phase…'

'Well, I'm not sure. We leave it outside the house and don't let it lie about in our room,' Mr Iqbal said, losing his patience.

'What? Is that how you treat your newly born granddaughter? I'm shocked beyond my wits, Mr Iqbal!' he said, turning red in the face and spitting out his words.

'Are you insinuating that this little mutt is my grandchild? Have you lost your mind, Mr Wilcox?' Mr Iqbal said, now furious, and with his blood pressure rising.

'Of course not! I'm talking about your elder daughter's fourth baby…'

'My elder daughter's fourth baby?'

'Indeed!'

'I didn't know she had had her first! My daughter got married three months ago. I think you need to lay off the whisky, Mr Wilcox. You probably have me mixed up with someone else,' Mr Iqbal said, taking his packet of hot buns. He handed over a few anna to Swami and briskly walked out of the door, with Rani following him, her tail wagging, as Mr Wilcox, now a shade of pink, watched them turn the corner and disappear.

◆

A week back

'Yes Aamir, come in. You've missed 5 days of school in the last two weeks. What, may I ask, is the reason?'

Aamir put his head down and averted his gaze from the Englishman's piercing glare.

'Sir, my sister just had a baby...'

'Already? Bloody hell! You don't say. But didn't she get married recently?'

'No sir, that's my older sister, this is the eldest. I have three sisters, sir,' Aamir said, naughtily holding up three fingers.

'And what, may I ask, do you have to do with her recent delivery?'

'Sir, my mother has been with her in hospital and we have three of her children to look after. She's had a baby every year, no sir?'

'Oh, is it?' he said, shaking his head in disbelief.

'Yes, the children are very small. I look after them, sir—I give them lunch and dinner and bathe them. Then my father got sick and he also went to the hospital, sir...'

'Oh my, that's a shame, you poor thing. So you're the brave young lad, eh? All right, go on then. Try not to miss class, young man,' he said, softening his tone. 'I love India, such strong family traditions, so well-knit, I must say. I'm proud of you, my boy!'

'Yes, sir,' Aamir said innocently before walking out of the room.

◆

Aamir walked into the Principal's office. Mr Wilcox was sitting there with a frown on his face, looking mortally upset.

'Sir, you called me?'

'Ah yes, so how's the family? Your newly born nephew, or was it niece?'

'Very good, sir. My sister had twins. She has five of them now. They grow up very fast.'

'Is it? It comes to me as a surprise, then, that your father is yet to learn of their existence. Now go and give your father this three-day suspension note,' he said, without emotion in his voice.

'Sir, why? Please sir, sorry. It won't happen again.'

'Well, you can look after your imaginary nephews and nieces, boy. Please leave now,' Mr Wilcox said, watching him walk out with tears running down his cheeks. He took out a bottle of whisky and poured himself a drink. Boys! he thought as he took a swig from his glass and sat back in his comfortable chair listening to the BBC on his radio.

The Music Room

IRA TRIVEDI

What was it about the end of winter days, about the beginning of spring, which was always too short, that always made him think of her? He took in the fragrance of the dying winter and the sweet smell of the dust, and for a second he held it in. If only this moment could last forever, the seamless transformation from winter to spring, when ochre pales to azure. He walked down the road to the music room, amongst the flippant cries of the students and the stamping of their little feet as they ran to their freedom when the last bell of the day had rung.

Suddenly, he was 17 again. He was walking as fast as possible, though he would sprint to her if he could. He couldn't do that; people would wonder where the head-boy was running to and it would draw unnecessary attention to himself since everyone on campus knew who he was. He had slipped her a note after lunch, asking her to see him. He would have to bunk Physics class when he probably should have attended it. Mr Matthews, the Physics teacher, had a distinctly pissed off look about him when he told him that he had to be excused from class on account of his head-boy duties. He dismissed him though he would have rather not. The trick always worked, and he rushed off to see her. The mere thought of her brought a light sweat to his freshly shaved upper lip. He could not wait to undo that sari, so much more graceful than lifting those sexless blue skirts and then hearing them complain later about how he had ruined the pleats. He was beyond skirts now; he had graduated to saris.

She was waiting for him in the Art Block, pretending to focus on stringing a violin. There was no way she could concentrate on anything right now, even if she was feeling a fraction of what he was. He saw her white bra, clearly visible underneath the thin yellow muslin blouse, and a shiver went down his spine. It turned him on. With her, everything was sex. The loose strands of her oily hair, the dust on her dainty, calloused feet, the small pimples on her cheek. Even thinking about her now, all these years later, unleashed a strong desire in his rusty self. He latched the heavy wooden door of the music room quietly and walked up to where she sat, putting his cold, sweaty palms on the softness of her stomach. She turned her head around shyly and laughed.

'You rascal, you're early.'

'I couldn't wait, Ma'am,' he said with a grin. 'I am an eager student, aren't I?' With that he began gently unfurling the bright, cheap pink sari that she wore, while she giggled and laughed with pleasure.

I'm not looking for elegiac or epiphanic moments; those are never the ones that inspire me. What brought me joy were just snatches and fragments of the life and rhythms of The Mewar Academy. Exactly fifty years ago, I was head-boy and today I am Head Master. Who would have ever imagined it? At every turn of the roads that I had recently rebuilt, there were memories. Memories of the youth that I had spent at this institution, memories from the years that my son had spent at this institution, and now, memories that I was gathering from being the Head Master of this school. Strangely, it was memories of her that brought back the most joy and also the most pain, and memories of her were always induced by the simplest of things.

The red munia, though nothing enchanting, was a bird that reminded me of her. It was also my favourite, simply because it was unappreciated. The munia is a musical bird, which is always short of breath and sings a discontinuous and feeble song. Yet, in its weakness there is a sweetness and endearing sadness. There is no more soothing a sound to me than the melodious, soft sound of the munia, for it will never cease to remind me of her.

I ran back from cricket practice, my impeccable whites stained with dark brown mud and with maroon blood from where the hard ball had hit me. I had watched her watch me from the side- lines, self-conscious in the midst of the other teachers. She would rather be with the crowds of raucous students; they were closer to her age anyway, but it was protocol for her to sit amongst all the staff and teachers. It's not like they paid any attention to her anyway. She was the music teacher and was at the very bottom of the totem pole. A majority of the teachers were British, the few Indian teachers mostly looked British, and all of them definitely behaved very British. She spoke English with a thick, provincial accent, and she knew the other teachers scoffed at her. The other Indian teachers wore thick, stylish silk saris with tastefully designed blouses. She felt cheap and garish in comparison and tried to avoid them completely. These days, she had even begun using the student's toilets so that she could avoid entering the enana, as she called the teachers' staffroom.

Her lover was an exhibitionist, he was garish and prodigal. He couldn't stop showing off the perfect control he wielded over the cricket bat. He was self-indulgent and exaggerated each victorious whack of the bat beyond the furthest limits of hyperbole, but none of it mattered, not at all. She had fallen in love with the boy who had cornered her and kissed her. She had been too nervous, scared and shy to say no to the roguish and handsome head-boy. He had simply put his arms around her as if she belonged to him, and all she could possibly do in his tight embrace was kiss him back. Before she knew it, all fear had melted and she found herself having a better time than she had ever had before. By now, she had learnt his likes and dislikes, peccadilloes and predilections, his mental makeup, the sound of his breath, his habits of love-making. She stood on the tips of her toes, trying to catch a glimpse of him. The crowds chanted his name and she smiled a shy smile. She would be chanting his name later that evening, albeit to a different taal.

We had lost the final and most important cup of the year, and it was only my fault. I was the only one to blame. I was, after all, the captain of the team and head-boy. It was I who should have led my team to victory, yet I had disappointed not only my team but the entire school, as well as the alumni body. I tried to internalize my calamity and give it some form of a heroic dimension but I found myself angry, sad and strangely violent. I couldn't be around anyone, but I also couldn't bear to be alone. I ran to the music room, flying at the speed of light, desperation and adrenaline making me work harder than I had during the entire match. I had to see her.

Where do violence and pain stop and sex start? Thoughts ravaged my mind and she lay next to me. Her beautiful, oily head on my chest, my hands cupped around her generous breasts. We lay amongst the dusty instruments, with nothing but a mouldy durri underneath us. She always made me feel better, this music teacher, red munia of mine, the kind, young, beautiful Ms Dutta. She was the only happy thing in my life these days. I was a glorious creature, leading the most glorious life, a life that anybody would have killed for. Every student on the campus aspired to be me. If only they knew what I was going through as I kept a calm, respectable aloofness that was expected of the head-boy, the fake permanent cheer and a false inspiring smile on my face. No one knew how much I loved her, how much I wanted to be with her, and how the thought of leaving her after graduation tormented every moment of my existence. Who would have thought that an innocuous stolen kiss one winter afternoon when I had practically forced myself on her would turn into this kind of brutal madness.

She is teaching me how to play the sitar, an unlikely musical instrument for someone like me, but even as a child, it was this instrument that I had loved. These days, I leave everything, my studies, my cricket practice, my head-boy duties, to practice. I want to become perfect, I want to please her. I imagine us making love to the tunes that I play, and I play and play and play, cutting into my hours of sleep to perfect a raga. My fingers no longer bleed as they used to and they are developing protective callouses that even my cricket bat hasn't managed to do. I think of my guru as I play, of her gentle instruction, of how she shakes her head when I strum the wrong note. When I throw my hands up in frustration, she advises me to be patient. The chin-chin of her bangles turns me on, and without any warning to myself or to her, I throw myself on her, tearing the thin blouse off her fragile frame.

'You rascal! The door isn't locked,' she gasps, though I see the twinkle in her almond eyes and I know I have not offended her. I run out of the room and twist the key in the heavy lock. We have devised an ingenious system of locking the front door from the outside, while we latch the back door from the inside, safely cocooned inside her heaven.

She is looking tired today, and there seem to be more of the rose-red pimples on her fair cheeks than there usually are. She looks worried, but I don't ask her anything, not because I don't want to, but because that is not our style. I don't want to embarrass her by asking her questions, or to make her self-conscious. Our conversations are always about me, my present, my future, my past. She seems thrilled and enamoured as I speak to her of my famous Rajput lineage and our grand customs, of the fort that is my home, and of the hunts that we go on every summer. I speak to her of my authoritative and regal father, of his three wives and many mistresses. She listens to me, a mixture of awe, glee and inspiration. She is transformed into a young child eagerly listening to the stories of a master. For this moment, I am her Guru and her God.

It seems that the past is with me every moment of my life. I am taking my daily rounds of the campus. As I walk past, all the workers and children become conscious and they sing out salutations, 'Good evening, sir', 'Good evening, sahib.' Suddenly, the chin-chin of the sweeper women's colourful glass bangles brings back memories with such strong force that I feel as if I have been punched hard in the gut. And then, once again, I am transported down memory lane.

She plays the sitar; her opening meditation is short but she more than makes up for it with her sinuous and subtle vilambit. I listen to her, a graceful creature if there ever was one. I watch her, her face a mask of pleasure, and then my attention goes to the glass bangles that she wears on her wrist. They create a musical chin-chin sound. I can't get my eyes off her fragile, dainty wrists, and the kaleidoscope of colours that envelop it. Something comes over me, maybe it is the music, or maybe it is her, but tears start pouring down my cheeks and I break into a sob. I haven't cried in years. Her meditation breaks and she looks up at me aghast. She comes running into my arms.

I play with the glass bangles on her wrist and she asks me if I would marry her. I don't know what to say, the cat has got my tongue, and it rarely ever does. I laugh, a laugh that sounds haughty and callous, though that is not what I am trying to be. Her face crumbles and the damage is already done. I have no idea what unspoken covenant I have broken, what unwritten law of nature I have transgressed, or in what way I have disappointed my joyous companion.

'Of course, my jaan. In my mind, we are already married. You are the only one that I will ever love.'

She turns around so I can't see her face, but when I touch her face, I feel the little beads of moisture streaming down her beautiful face.

This is the last memory I have of her. The heavy wooden door that we have ingenuously locked from the outside is cruelly broken down. We hear them trying, but they come in before she can put her sari on. We could not have escaped anyway, because there are people standing guard at the back door. It is a band of men, led by the Junior House Master, Mr Singh. They see her standing naked, with just her petticoat on, her breasts clearly visible through her thin blouse. One arm covers her chest, while the other holds her sari up. They come and take her away, not even letting her put her sari on. As for me, they don't touch me, but leave me standing there by myself. I'm paralyzed. I don't know if it is shock or fear, all I know is that I have never felt this way before. I stand there for a very long time, in that music room, on that mouldy durri, frozen in place. My black pants sitting loosely on my waist, unbuttoned, my shirt lying on the floor where she had carelessly flung it. On the floor lay several pieces of the pink and blue bangles that she had worn around her wrist. I collected the remnants of her, piece by piece. They were the only relics that I would have left of her.

I watched the scene unfold as if I was the spectator of a dark comedy of errors. I never saw her again after that day and no one else did either. They kicked her out of school on account of having an affair with a student. As for me, they did nothing to me. The Head Master called me into the office and gave me some sort of

a half-baked lecture, with a look of embarrassment on his face.
The irony was that, somehow, everyone seemed almost proud of
me. They winked at me and patted me on the back and whispered,
'Well done mate,' in my ear. I paid the price of my sins and the
vagaries of my mind, though not once did she leave me, images
of her haunting me constantly. I was ever fearful. I was fearful of
the fact that I had destroyed her life, and the thought of what I
had done to her plagued my soul every second of my existence.
Fear, unfortunately, is the most destructive of human emotions. It
corrodes the soul and the camaraderie it breeds is a false and forced
one. I quickly reverted to my old ways and habits, trying to get
involved with as much as I possibly could so that I could erase the
memory of the woman whom I had loved. People too were glad to
have me back. It's not that I didn't try to get in touch with her. I
tried very hard. I wrote her letters every day, sometimes I thought
that the letters were written more for me than they were for her.
All the letters, every single one of them, came back undelivered. I
had no way of getting in touch with her again. I told myself that I
would find her once I graduated and was out of the claustrophobic
confines of the Academy.

The day after graduation, when I came home, I found a bride
waiting for me on my doorstep. I was engaged, as was the custom
of my family, to an appropriate girl. I was then quickly whisked
off to London to finish my studies.

It is rather strange, but I still feel a sort of repulsion when
my wife wears glass bangles around her wrists. The first time she
did, when we were newly married, I made her take them off and
I broke each one of them, the red shards of glass mixing with the
red of my blood. Then there was the time when she wore a white
bra with a thin, pink muslin blouse. I was so angry that I could
have murdered her that very instant. I reprimanded her severely

and told her that only classless women exposed themselves like that, and if I ever saw her bra through her blouse again, she would have it from me.

I never did have the chance to look for her the way that I should have, the way that I had promised myself I would on the day that she disappeared. She had left my life as quickly as she had appeared. Soundlessly, without a twang of the sitar, or the chin-chin of her glass bangles.

Welcome to St. Gibbs

AHMED FAIYAZ

V ikrant quietly crept into the classroom and walked towards the second row, near the door where he saw an empty desk. He noticed many eyes sizing him up, probably wondering where he came from. He averted his gaze, keeping his eyes on the floor, and refused to make eye contact with any of the backbenchers.

He noticed some of them smiling at him, and one of them even pointed at him. *I'm done for!* he thought. While his family had recently moved from Chennai, he was in a way glad to leave his old school where he was bullied no end. Daffy and Moon-face were the names he was popularly addressed by. The boys back in Sherwood laughed, either looking at his face or hearing him talk. *I'm going to keep my mouth shut,* he told himself.

'Hi, I'm Rahul,' the boy wearing Gandhi-style spectacles said with a broad smile.

'Hi ... I'm Vikrant,' he said nervously, at which Rahul snickered.

'Do you have a sore throat?'

Vikrant shook his head. His heart skipped a beat.

'These guys from the back bench are going to lay it on you. Stay clear of them, they're very mean!'

'Do they trouble you as well?'

'Last week, they poured ink on my head,' he said with a sad face.

'But now that you're a new boy here, they should take it easy on me.'

'I hope they don't,' Vikrant muttered. He was sweating now and dreaded being ragged on his first day. He turned around to see four boys taller than him staring at him from the last bench. All of them smiled at him and one of them even waved.

'Stop turning back, you're in trouble,' Rahul hissed. 'They'll probably throw you in the dustbin at lunch.'

'What?'

'Yes. The teacher is here, stand up.'

Vikrant could pay little attention in class. He raised his hand when the roll call was being taken and quietly dreaded the lunch break. *I'll go and hide in the bathroom,* he thought.

On hearing the bell for lunch a few classes later, he stood up to rush out of the class when a tall, chubby kid stepped in his path.

'Oh God! You're in for it,' Rahul mumbled.

'You're the new boy, right?' he asked in a friendly voice.

Vikrant nodded and kept his head down.

'You've recently moved from Chennai, right?' he asked.

Vikrant nodded again and looked up. The rest of the gang stood around him.

'I'm Rajiv, and these are Sid, Achal and Abrar,' he said pointing his chubby fingers at each of them.

'You've recently moved into Shanti Homes, haven't you?' the boy called Sid asked. He appeared to Vikrant as the most intimidating.

Vikrant nodded again. *They even know where I live. Shit!*

'I live in Shanti Manor, across the street from your building. 102A. I saw your family move in last week,' the boy called Achal said, smiling at Vikrant.

'Hey biscuit, what's for lunch?' Sid curtly asked Rahul who was trying to walk away unnoticed.

'Nothing…Just a couple of chicken rolls, Sid,' he said meekly.

'And you're trying to escape,' Rajiv said, staring down at him.

'Open the box. What are you waiting for, little biscuit?' Abrar said.

'Here,' Rahul said, handing over his box which was grabbed at by Rajiv.

'Why don't we offer some to our new friend here?' Achal said to the others.

'Yes, eat, eat...You must. We're friends after all,' Sid said slapping Vikrant's back.

'Thank you,' Vikrant said, putting his hand into Rahul's box with some hesitance. He saw Rahul turn pale as he stood there watching the others devour his lunch.

'Go drink some Bournvita, little biscuit,' Sid snickered. He was taller than the rest of them and had long, curly hair.

'So Vikrant...We'll call you Vicky...How was class? You like your new school?' Rajiv asked, speaking with his mouth full.

'It's okay,' Vikrant said. He was sweating now, wondering what their game was with him.

'You don't worry about anything in this school. You're our friend; join the gang,' Sid said holding his hand out for a handshake.

Vikrant shook his hand with his sweaty palm, realizing how strong his grip was.

'Sid here is the track star. He's the 100 metres and 200 metres champion. No one can outrace him. He also opens the batting for the junior cricket team,' Abrar said.

'Now you're one of us. Come sit on the last bench. Leave little biscuit here to his Livingstone and Wordsworth,' Achal said. 'You're my neighbour also man, let us know if you need any help.'

Rahul looked surprised and Vikrant's face lit up.

'How about some ice cream? I'm going to get some,' Rajiv announced.

'Let's get our new friend a Feast,' Sid announced and put his arm around him.

'Or do you want a cone of ice cream?' Abrar asked.

'Don't mess with our friend huh, little biscuit? You'll bring him lunch tomorrow,' Achal said, at which Rahul nodded meekly, while Sid walked ahead with Vikrant.

'We'll help you with anything you need huh, Vikrant,' the bespectacled Abrar added.

'We'll come over and help you unpack,' Rajiv grunted.

'You have any gaming console?' Abrar asked, before he tapped on his shoulder.

'Nintendo,' Vikrant blurted out.

'Good, we'll play some games then,' Achal said with a broad smile.

'Yes, we'll unwind at your place. After all, we're friends now,' Sid said.

◆

Vikrant walked into his room with a wide grin. 'What are you smiling about? How was your first day?' his older sister Vidya asked. She sounded irritable and tired. Like him, she had changed schools and was having a hard time. She was 18 months older than him, and a year senior to him in school.

'Very good, I made a lot of new friends! They're very nice to me,' he beamed.

'Really? Nice,' she said. 'I wish the girls at St. Anne's were as nice. They were so bitchy and snooty!'

They heard the doorbell. 'Please open the door na, didi. I'll go and change,' he said.

'Who is it now? At this time?'

'I think it's the gang from class. I asked them to come over and play on my Nintendo.'

'Oh God! Please keep them in the living room. I'm reading, I don't want to be disturbed.'

'Yes didi, now get the door will you?'

'Going baba,' she said, walking out of the room.

◆

'I hope I get to meet her,' Sid grinned as he stood outside Vikrant's apartment.

'Yes, I hear she's really beautiful!' Rajiv said.

'I'm the one who told you,' Achal added.

'I hope she talks to me too,' Abrar said.

'How's my hair?' Sid asked, while running his fingers through his gelled-back hair.

'Nice,' Rajiv said nervously, tucking his tummy in. 'Better than that joker Vikrant's hairstyle.'

'Yeah, imagine, for a funny lad like that, his sister is a goddess,' Achal said before they heard the latch on the main door open.

Smells Like Home

AASHISH MEHROTRA

20th May: the date stamp annoyed me as I scrolled through the list to look for movies on my in-flight entertainment system, but I couldn't concentrate on the list of films as my eyes kept going back to the date that was flashing on the top right corner of the screen. The date really had no significance in my past, not much of a past is left behind by a 15-year-old anyway. I had been avoiding this day since my parents told me we were shifting to Bombay for good.

I gave up my search for a good movie to watch and fumbled through my pockets, hoping to find something that would entertain me for another hour till we landed. I struggled with my seatbelt and tried to empty my pockets. Halfway through the process, I felt my mother's piercing glare on me. I looked to my right and she was sitting there with her headphones on and her Bollywood movie on pause. I saw Govinda on the screen gyrating to some music with Raveena Tandon for company. My Mum scolded me to sit properly and keep quiet. I looked at what I could pull out of my pocket and stared at my boarding pass, a few candy wrappers, rubber bands and my passport. I couldn't help but feel disgust when I looked at my passport. It was the only thing that really proved I was Indian. None of my features could reveal my ethnicity—I was a green eyed, fair skinned, tall lad, with an Australian accent, and could easily pass off as Steve Waugh's distant cousin. I tucked my passport away and stared long and hard at the boarding pass.

Sydney to Bombay—a one-way ticket. I suddenly felt really sick.

The only thing I was excited about at that moment was getting to crib about the famous Bombay stench. I walked towards the exit of the plane, took one step forward, closed my eyes and took a deep breath. Before I could crib about it, my mother pulled me towards the immigration line cribbing about my 'attitude problem'.

'You better change Ajay, this behaviour won't work in Indian schools you know,' she grumbled.

'I just want to go home Mom, I don't want to live in India. This place stinks,' I moved away from her and stood in one place, not wanting to go further.

'You are home now, Ajay. This is home, this is where we have to make our lives.' *Really? Damn.*

I walked up to the sour-faced immigration officer, who showed me his paan-stained teeth, while thinking about the rugby match that Scott, Shane and rest of the boys were to play today.

♦

It had been a week since we moved to Bombay, and I was yet to muster the courage to step out of the house. The crowds, the noises, the beggars were all so alien to me. The day I dreaded the most, the first day of school, was upon me. I reluctantly stood in front of what I was told was my 'school'. I stared at the ramshackle building in front of me. It looked like a rundown mill, the windows had bars on them and the ground floor of the building housed grocery stores, a travel agent and a butcher's shop. The top three floors were supposed to be my school—according to my mother, that is. To me, it looked like they were locking me up in an asylum. At that moment, I wondered, *have I actually gone crazy?* Is it just me, who thinks going to school feels like being forced into a mental asylum?

The only reasons I had to go to this school were its proximity to where we lived, and the fact that I didn't speak much Hindi. My mother's paranoia had led me here, where I would be spending half of my day above a butcher's shop. 'It's my home away from home,' I said to myself with mock sarcasm as I rolled my eyes.

I walked up to the third floor and looked at the map to find my assigned classroom. Noisy kids were running in the hallway. Some of them were dangerously kicking about a football in the narrow passage for want of a soccer field. I dodged the ball and soon stood outside my new classroom. I just couldn't muster the strength to walk in. I wanted to turn around and run back home to my room. Not the 10×10 jail cell here they make me believe is my room. The one I left behind in Sydney where my closet was as big as what they called a classroom here.

I opened the door to the classroom, closed my eyes and took a deep breath. The smell of impending doom swept in on me. It smelt just like lavender with a little hint of nuts. *What is this?* I thought.

'Are you ok? You look nauseated,' I heard someone say.

I opened my eyes and found myself staring, not into someone's eyes, but a neck, a long neck followed by the most gorgeous collar-bone I had ever seen.

'Are you new here?' she asked, followed by the most perfect smile.

Oh boy. I snapped out of my trance, inflicted by a combination of lavender, nuts and, most amusingly, a neck. I sensed a hundred eyes that glared at me with interest.

'I'm new here,' I replied with the dumbest look on my face.

My gaze shifted from her neck to her smile to her eyes—small and beautiful, hazel with a caramel outer ring. It's funny how you can notice the most detailed things about most people when you've met them only for a few seconds. In those few seconds, standing at the doorway, I gaped at this most beautiful woman before me. I could swear that it felt like I had been staring at her for hours. Suddenly, the dilapidated school around me didn't feel like a mental asylum.

Before I knew it, she beckoned me gently to a seat in the front of the classroom. My heart beat grew louder as I kept thinking, rather hoping, she was going to sit next to me. My first day in my new school and I meet such a gorgeous classmate, it just felt unreal. I sat down at the desk offered and looked up at the girl.

She walked to the blackboard and all I could hear were her footsteps and the sound of her skirt against the air blowing in from the window. She wrote something in block letters on the board. It took me 5 seconds, but once I read the board everything crashed into me like a tsunami wave, destroying everything in sight.

The classroom was noisy, with people throwing things, while they chattered loudly using a mix of Hindi and English, and the smell, I couldn't even describe it, it wasn't lavender anymore. I read the board once more. Miss Sethna: Substitute Hindi teacher, it said.

I suddenly felt a lot of pain. I didn't know why there was a sharp pain in my shin.

'Oww. What the hell?' I grunted.

I looked to my right and a girl with two ponytails giggled at me, 'Pass it on, no returns,' she said controlling her giggles.

I looked at her puzzled, 'Why did you kick me?'

She now looked equally puzzled, as she had already given her reason for kicking me hard in the shin.

'Aree, pass it on, no return,' she repeated in her sweet raspy voice as if I didn't hear it the first time.

'What is this?'

She broke into a fit of giggles again, looking at the confused expression on my face.

I ignored her, just as I ignored all other sights and sounds, and continued to gape at Miss Sethna. It made all the pain go away, even the pain in my shin from the kick, and that in my head from the cackle of geese next to me. Everything just felt better.

Before I knew it, the bell rang and Miss Sethna left, taking the whiff of lavender fragrance with her. She left me alone to deal with the noise, the pain in my shin and the noisy brood in this fish market.

I sat alone during lunch and just stared at my food, not feeling hungry at all. The girl who kept kicking me in class came and sat next to me, and as a reflex action carefully I moved my foot out of kicking range. She laughed, 'Don't worry, I won't hurt you, silly!'

I still didn't share her sense of humour. She started chattering about how fried chicken was her favourite food, and blue was her favourite colour. I just stared blankly at her. She wasn't the prettiest girl, and had a long mop of curly hair which she tried to manage by tying it up in plaits. There was something about the twinkle in her black eyes that kept my attention as she chattered on and on. She gesticulated merrily, almost dancing in her chair as she spoke, and kept rocking her chair. She just couldn't sit still. My patience only broke when she reached her second great-grandfather who fought in the independence struggle in the 1940s.

'Is there a reason you are telling me all this?'

She blinked and looked at me. I expected her to get up and leave as I had rudely interrupted her narration of the freedom struggle.

'You are new here, silly and I'm trying to make you feel at home,' she said flashing her pearly whites at me. I found myself smiling at her goofily for a moment.

'This place can never feel like home. The horrid smell just…' I trailed off.

I looked at this girl sitting in front of me, smiling at me and waiting, wanting to listen to what I had to say next and I realised that I knew her grandfather's name was Amarnath but I couldn't seem to remember hers.

'I am Ajay,' I said, perking up a bit and changing my tone.

Her eyes opened wide and her smile widened. 'My name is Karishma,' she said while trying to control her giggling.

Her warmth and her efforts to cheer me up just made me smile.

It was short-lived, for I felt a sudden pain in my shin. Still smiling, she looked at me. 'Pass it on, no returns,' she said while sticking her tongue out.

The next day I left home and found Karishma sitting on a bench outside my house. She got up looking irritated, 'It's about time, silly. We are going to be late for class.'

I just stood there till she dragged me by the arm. Baffled, I looked at her wondering what to say, 'How did you know where I stay?'

She just giggled at the question like it was one of the dumbest things I could've asked. As we walked to school, she hopped and jumped around merrily, being almost a foot shorter than me. I thought it was rather amusing for the people around us to watch her jumping around me, a giant in comparison. She kept on about the places we passed, waving to tea-stall vendors, milk men on their cycles, and even the pigeons fluttering around. I couldn't help but laugh at her cute insanity.

We both got separated in class because I was put into another division as I was behind in most of the subjects, especially Hindi. Karishma just couldn't understand my excitement when I was told that I would be getting after class tuitions from Miss Sethna to improve my Hindi.

The after-class lessons were the best 45 minutes of my life. It was just me and Miss Sethna alone, with her voice echoing in the empty classroom. Somehow she made Hindi sound sweeter.

After every class ended, I would find Karishma waiting for me to walk me home.

As the days passed, our walk back home became longer and longer. Karishma would tell me about her day and I would talk about my classes with Miss Sethna. Karishma would talk to me about all the 'hip and happening' Hindi slang and I would regale her with stories about Sydney and how clean the air was, how the smell of barbeques in private lawns would fill the air on Sundays.

Months passed, and one day while walking to school I noticed Karishma was less chirpy than usual and wore a forced smile. She walked slowly, a step or two behind me, and she avoided making eye contact. There was something so different about her. She had not tied her hair in the usual way, she had cut it nicely and straightened it, her clothes seemed shorter and there was something on her face. There was an awkward silence between us. Missing the jumpy and jovial Karishma, and unable to take the silence, I nudged her.

'Is everything okay?' I asked.

She shrugged her shoulders, 'Everything is fine.' She had a faraway look in her eyes.

I remained silent. When we were just about reaching school she looked at me for the first time that morning and asked, 'Why do you like Miss Sethna so much?'

The question caught me off guard. Frankly, at that point I didn't have an answer. I just looked at her with a blank expression, while thinking of why I liked Miss Sethna. Then it struck me what made Karishma look so different from her usual bouncy and no frills self.

'Karishma, do you have makeup on your face?' I asked with some hesitation.

She bit her lip and averted her gaze away from mine. Tears welled up in her eyes and caused a stream of mascara to roll down her cheek. I just stood there and watched Karishma pull away from me and run inside school.

I sat in class thinking about the past few months with Karishma, us getting wet in the rain, eating golas and sipping Thumbs Up and Goldspot after gorging on spicy Pav Bhaji. I remembered how she would try to make me laugh whenever I was low, our long walks and longer conversations. Most of which were about me and my after-school classes with Miss Sethna.

I suddenly felt like an idiot. I hadn't even noticed Karishma trying to garner my attention every day, trying to impress me hold my attention and distract me whenever I raised the topic of how wonderful Miss Sethna was. I had actually driven her to wearing shorter skirts and applying hideous amounts of makeup.

I stood outside the door, waiting for Miss Sethna's after-school class. For the first time, I was dreading it. I didn't want to sit in class and learn Hindi. I didn't want to hear her melodious voice, I just wanted to find Karishma and talk to her. I reluctantly stepped inside the classroom, only to find it empty. I had decided to tell Miss Sethna that I liked Karishma and not her, and to please excuse me for today.

I looked around the whole school, but I couldn't find her. I stepped outside in the cold winter air and, on my way towards the sports room, I saw Miss Sethna in the arms of a burly man, hugging her, with his arms around her waist. Before he leaned in to kiss her, I turned around. The cold air started pinching my lungs and I struggled to catch my breath. She turned around to find me standing there and she rushed up to me.

'Sorry Ajay, there's no class today, I have to leave. I hope you understand,' she said in a sheepish voice. She had a dreamy expression on her face and her cheeks were flushed.

I just stood there looking at her and then at the beefy man, our games master, who stood there with a bouquet of flowers, impatiently awaiting her return. I decided to remain silent and not acknowledge her.

Miss Sethna looking rushed, and looking beyond my shoulders, asked, 'Ajay, is everything alright?'

I looked up to her and forcing a smile said, 'Everything's fine, Miss.'

Then I just stood there, watching flabbergasted, as she sat in the car and drove off with Mr Pal, holding on to the flowers she had just received. All the months of trying to grab her attention, being her best student, applying gel in my hair and always complimenting her had gone in vain. She didn't even notice me or think of me in the same light. I probably came across as some affectionate, eccentric, goofy kid from Australia. *What an idiot I've been!*

But I also felt a deep sense of relief. I suddenly turned and started looking around wildly. *Where is she? Where is Karishma?* I needed to talk to her, I needed my best friend. I decided that she would come back and we would go back to being normal like the old times. So I just stood there in front of my school, my home away from home, waiting for her laughter to ring in my ears. The school once again started to look like a rundown mill, the smell of Bombay in the cold started hurting my senses. It just wasn't home anymore; it felt like the first day when I had stood in front of the structure and felt nothing but hate. Only, this time, I hated myself.

I lay awake at night, not being able to sleep without my dose of Karishma's gossip, chatter and giggles. I counted the hours, minutes and seconds to morning light. I got ready as fast as I could and opened my door. I stood there looking right into the eyes of the newspaper boy.

'Sir, your school starts at 8 na? It is only 7…'

I looked past him, hoping to find Karishma waiting for me as always, only to look at an empty bench. I couldn't believe it. All this while I hadn't noticed her, and now I had lost the one person I cared about in this whole place. I went and sat on the bench, hugging my backpack to keep myself warm.

My mother came and sat down next to me on the bench, milk bottles and a newspaper in one hand, and a sweater in the other. She wrapped the sweater around me and just sat there without saying a word.

'Mum, I'm an idiot!'

She gave me a knowing look and smiled, while I waited for her comforting words and pearls of wisdom.

'That you are sometimes. What happened?'

I looked at her and she looked expectantly back at me. We both burst into laughter.

She hugged me and whispered, 'The fact that you realise you're an idiot will make you wiser.'

'Mum, that doesn't make sense.'

'Do you want go back home to Sydney, son?'

I looked at my school in the distance and then back at my mother.

I smiled and shook my head. I got up, 'I am home, Mom.'

I grabbed my backpack and rushed down the road towards school. I ran past the tea-stall waving to the stall owner as I rushed past. Going past the butcher's shops, grocery stores and travel agents, I yelled 'good morning' to them all.

For some reason I knew where I had to go. I ran to the mess hall and stopped. In the corner of the hall, sitting with her head down and nothing but her now nicely done let-loose-about-her-shoulders hair showing, was Karishma. I quietly went and sat down next to her.

'Karishma, I am an idiot. I don't know what to say and how to say it. Yesterday, when I had to go to Miss Sethna's class I was actually dreading it. I didn't want to go, I just wanted to meet you, hear your laughter and see you smile. I don't want you to wear makeup or do anything stupid. After cribbing about this place for nearly a year now, this place is finally…You made this place… Karishma, without you I just feel like…'

I suddenly felt a pain in my shin. I rubbed it and Karishma slowly looked up at me with a twinkle in her eye.

I brushed strands of her hair away from her cheeks, wiped her tears, and then drew my lips to hers.

I looked at her with a broad grin, 'Don't pass it on, but returns are welcome.'

Karishma looked at me, surprised by my move, and then lunged towards me, collapsing in my arms and hugging me tightly.

Stroking her hair, I hugged her back and whispered, 'You made this my home, silly girl…'

One Bump Does No Harm

NAMAN SARAIYA

Every night as he lay down beside her, playing with her hair, stroking his fingers against her cheek and watching her sleep peacefully, a sense of disbelief came over him. As he looked into her eyes, as she slightly opened them, lying beside her, the glint in her eyes blinded his doubts and assured him of their future together. They had never seen a shaky moment together but once, during their school days when he had been caught in an awkward situation with another girl. But he recovered soon. His conscience made sure he did, for he had already promised Izna a life together—a life filled with gaiety and contentment.

It was the winter of 2001 when he walked into the tutorial classes that he detested, not for anything else, but the fact that he didn't require any help in the English language. Nonetheless, being a Mamma's boy, he never argued and kept going back, again and again—only to have gradually grown fond of the environment and the fact that his snobbery would lead him to pick on whomever he liked. He was aware of this and, well, didn't care much for it. That obviously did not go down too well with the other students—who mostly had nothing to say to him. It was here that he first saw her, in the first year of their high school. But the beginning of their story had not been the most pleasant.

Izna. Oh, what a name. He couldn't help but keep repeating it in his head, in different tones and scales, almost as if it were a magic spell. Well, it did cast a spell on him, though he tried hard to not make that evident. The kohl-laden eyes, the perfectly tied hair and the loose shirts she wore, all garnered his attention and kept pulling him back, time after time—not only to her, but also to the tutorials. And the tutor, almost like his Godmother, was beginning to sense the situation and never stopped him from doing what he must. This was beginning to interest him. And how did he first speak to her?

'It's pasta, not paezta. It's pronounced pasta!' What a dud! He had to get over correcting everyone's grammar all the bloody time.

Next time, she smirked as he walked in, but he let it pass and smiled back with a warm hello. He knew the others in the room were surprised at his strange warmth that evening, but he gathered his act together quickly and got back to business, pulling someone's leg or being sarcastic. His Godmother had often referred to his nasty sarcasm and said, 'One day you will cut someone up with your razor sharp tongue.' He often grinned back and claimed to have learnt all of it from her. Mind you, she was polite when needed, but as they say, if you can't take the heat, don't tickle the dragon. That evening, he walked Izna back to her car, only to receive strange vibes, not only from her but also her chauffeur.

Something inside him said she was the one. And well, he made sure he had a plan, regardless of never having followed it. He always goofed up while attempting to make over-smart statements, stepping on objects while walking her out, spilling coffee while looking at her and not writing a word about Macbeth's character, instead writing how he felt looking at her. This more or less defined his school evenings from then on, but there was more to it than met the eye. She was believed to have been the rationalist who, for once, had given in—and how. But the art of covering it up had made her unreadable and even more mysterious. Then again, he had his sources and he knew how exactly he was to get around this case, though the lack of any form of experience bothered him.

That particular balmy evening in their final year at high school was a special one. By now, a few weeks had passed, but despite making matters very obvious, neither side had made a move. Teenage love was always confusing and dreamy—and she wanted to give it some thought. So, that balmy evening in September, she went over to his place with the excuse of collecting some notes and discussing a few important questions lined up for the examinations ahead. There was an unreal shudder running down his body as he saw her walk through the gate and it worsened as the doorbell rang. He ran to the door, stood in front of it for a few seconds and opened it slowly, smiling like a fool. The cold marble flooring, the emptiness in the pit of his stomach and the discomfort—all perfect.

He did a little jig as she walked up the stairs and followed her up, then leading her into the room. After handing over the notes that he had carefully compiled, he pulled a chair for her and they sat to work out some answers. She asked where his mother was, to which he said she had been out of town for over a week now. He spotted a faint smile on her face on the reception of his answer. Then she held his hand and put it on the notes and giggled in excitement, asking him to get to work since they had a lot to do. This was the most expressive he had seen her since he had gotten to know her and that somehow excited him. Going over Macbeth, the sun went down.

In the process, he made her some coffee, which was rather good, she said a couple of years later. All through the process of him stirring up what he thought was an aphrodisiac, she smiled to herself thinking of how she had landed up in such a situation. She took both the cups as he approached her and placed them on the kitchen platform behind her. He realized he was at an uncomfortably close distance from her, something that had never happened in their weeks of knowing each other. He stood still, feet jammed to the ground and a gazillion thoughts rushing through his head all at once. And then, all of a sudden, she looked up straight into his eyes—the way he would, later, in the future, and said to him, 'Do you think I'm stupid?' He tried to speak, but no words were heard. Before he realized it, her nose was touching his and their eyelids were batting against each other's. He had not done this before, ever. In retrospect, he was pretty impressive, she said.

He often recalled the incident and narrated a slightly toned down version to his friends at reunions and otherwise, and followed it up with the cheesy, 'The rest, as they say, is history.' Thereafter, he often told her she was the light of his life to which she asked why and his instant reply was, 'Your name means it.' Being on school campus was more fun, since she could be found around. He often wondered how he had never noticed her earlier, in all those years. He consoled himself with the fact that it was probably because she was quiet and had always been in the other section. Being a School Prefect gave him the liberty of pulling her out of class whenever, though he restricted it to the times when the urge to see her was unbearable.

Towards the last few days of school, after everyone had left, they found themselves alone in the Music Room, located in one corner of the school field. The vastness of the campus had never seemed like a blessing earlier and, this time around, he had no words to express how he felt. The high ceiling, the ancient fans, the smelly white paint, the wooden desks and their markings—everything seemed like an undreamt fantasy. He darted a mischievous look to her across the room and she signalled no. He approached the door, locked it and closed all the windows, shutting the world outside. He then pinned her to the blackboard and as she told him, at a later date, he was at the top of his game that afternoon.

He went back home after the last day of school and looked at all the photographs that had been clicked by his camera and realized some of the best pictures of Izna and him were the ones from that day. A couple of them had even found a place on the walls of their home and one particular picture, on the bedside table. However, there was also one picture of his...one with Rhea Sharma...Rhea Sharma had been a friend of his since forever and had been rather pleased and supportive of his and Izna's burgeoning relationship. What Rhea felt uneasy about, was that one incident...that one secret they shared, that she would never share with Izna, for his sake.

At a party, the night before the last day of school, Izna had not showed up for some reason. He had gotten pretty drunk on an excessively large share of alcohol and Rhea was to take him back home. Not drinking that night and being the rich kid that she was, she had brought her car and decided to drop her friend back home. Somewhere along the way, the car found itself on a deserted road and he spoke of how he loved Izna and how they were going to the same college. As he blabbered on, he suddenly found himself in a compromising situation with someone who had been his best friend. He was aware of what was happening, but didn't know whether to stop or keep going. He did stop her eventually because felt it was wrong. No words were spoken after that till she dropped him back home. As he left the car, she told him that she had always wanted it to happen, but it wouldn't, ever. A promise kept.

After their final board examinations there was lot of crying and final goodbyes were bid. This was not the end of the world and he had known this and behaved it as well, but after what had happened that night, he was more than glad to be seeing some people for the last time. He mentioned though that he was not running away from the situation, because he hardly remembered any of it, but because it gave him a sense of closure. From then onwards, he led a life that was devoid of a lot of memories created on campus, with friends and otherwise, but selectively picked the ones with Izna and guarded them with all his heart.

Years passed, and Izna and he were still together. College flew by just fine and a fresh bunch of memories on a new campus were created along with some more people. Some of those people stuck by, some moved on just like some from the previous campus did. Life had its way of healing open wounds and sealing them with the help of time and newer situations. He often felt that it was for both their sakes that he had kept this secret from Izna. His conscience was clear, as clear as crystal—because to err is human, but to suffer because of another's erring is unfair.

That night, he drank a little extra coffee. Going through his cupboard, he took out the album that had their school photographs and removed all the ones featuring Rhea. *Sometimes, honesty is not the best policy*, he reassured himself. But then again, lying was also not the best option. In his opinion, he had not lied, but just hidden what had made them stronger in years to come. Convinced of his conscience being clear, he burnt the photographs secretly, as Izna slept. He crawled back into bed late and kissed her forehead, thus waking her up. She asked him what had happened to him all of a sudden. He said he had to ask her a question, a very important one: What happens if he speeds the car over a road bump?

A bit taken aback, she replied, 'Well, one bump never really does any harm.'

That's It?

SAHIL KHAN

Screwed! What the hell was I thinking when I broke the CD reflector in two? Zoeb, you're unbelievably stupid!

Zoeb had just been dragged into the Vice Principal's office by a teacher who'd self-appointed herself the Discipline in-Charge.

Crime? That Zoeb was carrying a blue film. After quite a spat with the teacher in the corridor over who was right about the subject of suspension and putting up an enjoyable show for his fellow 8th graders, Zoeb was now standing in front of the VP.

Vadapav. Hate him to the guts. Feel like tying his long hairy beard to the drawer and whacking his head till he starts bleeding and is lying on the floor, unconscious.

The teacher, furious, was throwing light on the incident and was giving Zoeb the how-dare-you look. The VP, though listening to her, was staring hard at Zoeb, for he could finally add his name to the list. He asked the peon to get a plain sheet of paper which was placed in front of Zoeb. As the forced confession was written out, photocopied and filed, there was a certain glee on the VP's face. Zoeb was asked to head back to the class and wait for further notice from the office.

As the last class of the day was coming to an end, a peon came in, gave an envelope to the class teacher and left. Zoeb was called out to collect it and sign a receipt. As he signed it, Zoeb requested the teacher to let him attend the classes while not marking him present. He went back to his desk.

How am I going to tell Dad? Chhodo, bhaad mein jaaye. The teacher's anyway okay with me sitting in class. Keep a low profile for the next three days and we should be sorted.

The last bell rang, indicating the end of the day. As the rest of the students hurried off to catch their bus back home, Zoeb stayed back to hide the suspension letter in the teacher's cabinet. His mom had a habit of going through his bag once in a while.

Darn, getting late. Run. Two at a time. Jump the last four. Skid. Change angle. Two at a time. Jump the last three. Change angle. Run down the corridor, into the lobby, out the main gate and towards the school bus.

By the time he had hopped in to his bus, the other guys in the bus had already got the word out about Zoeb's suspension. Zoeb was lucky enough to persuade his sister into not sharing this piece of news at home for a bunch of Cadbury Dairy Milks.

The next day, no matter how out-of-the-scene Zoeb tried to be, seniors and other batch mates came by to show support to him and were happy that someone had bothered to stand up to the self-centred bitch of a teacher.

The day otherwise would've ended uneventfully, but Zoeb managed to find himself a new interest.

Two at a time. Jump the last four. Skid. Change angle. Two at a time. Jump the last three. Change angle. Run down the corridor, into the lobby... Stop. Glance. Cute. Look at watch. Sprint.

Halfway through the second day of suspension and still attending school, Zoeb now didn't worry about calling his father to meet the teachers. He was more keen on trying to figure out who the cute girl whom he had noticed the previous day in the lobby was. He eagerly waited for school to end.

1.43 p.m. Can't see her. Walk out to look for her. Nope. Go back in. There she is. Talking to a friend. Walk up to them. No. Wait. She's leaving. Hmm.

Day 3 of the suspension taught Zoeb never to get his hopes up. The VP, during his rounds, noticed Zoeb sitting in the class. Obviously, he was called out and when Zoeb tried to argue with the VP as to how he'd been wrongly incriminated and hence would not ask his parents to come meet him, he was quietly sent to the Principal's office.

'I have told the Principal you're coming to his office. He will only sort this issue out now,' and blah, blah, blah. Dadhiyal saala. Wonder which one of those cars is his. Someone should let the air out from the tyres. Saale ka ladka khud tamaashe karta hai, chala hai doosron ko suspend karne.

The Principal, the sweet chap that he was, was never happy about such incidents, but was particularly unhappy as he knew Zoeb's father personally. And this was troubling Zoeb as well. He knew, this time, that he didn't have a way out.

The considerate Principal heard Zoeb's version and then the VP's. The computer lab assistant was called in to see if the broken reflector could somehow be checked for its apparent contents, but no such luck. Zoeb was asked to spend the rest of day in the parents' waiting room and get his father to come meet the Principal the next day.

Four hours to kill! Why didn't I issue a book during the last library period! Grr. Let's go check who's on the basketball court.

With another 15 minutes or so left for the last period to get over, Zoeb took a deep breath, picked up his bag and headed towards the lobby. He wanted to find out who that girl was. The thought of having his Dad visit the Principal wasn't bothering him right now.

Should go talk to her. No. Umm. Chhod na. Hmm, wait for her to leave. Go find her name out from the friend. Oh no, what if the friend leaves first? Okay, relax. Take a deep breath.

Very much like *Just Mohabbat* on Sony Entertainment Television, Zoeb was in luck as the friend was the one who stayed back. He managed to get her name from the friend. Found out her class as well. Disha. VII B. Zoeb wondered if her friend would tell her about the incident. What would her reaction be? Not positive for sure. Inquisitive? He hoped so.

I'm home now. Should I go talk to Dad about the whole suspension thing right now? Maybe I'll tell him in the morning before leaving for school… this way I'll reduce the severity of his reaction as he will be distracted by the fact of having to meet the principal. Hmm, smart!

Zoeb spent the evening looking for Disha in the previous school magazines, wondering if she liked writing, played sports, had won any awards or topped her class. Finding nothing on her, he cajoled his kid sister to snoop around the next day at school. Post-dinner, he realized that a daunting task was to be executed in the morning.

Dad, I was suspended for… No, but I didn't… Argh, Zoeb, rehearse, rephrase again. The phone's ringing? Must be the hospital calling for an on-call visit. Dammit, lesser time. Hang on, the bus isn't coming? Yippee, no school! No wait, oh crap, Dad's dropping us off? Hmm… More time to rehearse.

As Zoeb's sister ran into the campus, he was still forming his opening line. What hit him next came as a surprise. His father was scolding him, not for being suspended, but for informing him about the meeting with the Principal when he was standing right outside the school in a T-shirt and sandals! A rather perplexed Zoeb quietly led the way to the Principal's office.

Festivals, Elections & Placements

Loves Me, Loves Me Not

VIBHA BATRA

Today is the worst day of my life. You see, there is a girl I love. Very much. And she won't even spare me a second glance. Most of the time she acts like I don't even exist. But if she thinks that not acknowledging me will make my love go away, she is wrong.

This has been going on for a year now, right since the first day of college. But today is the worst day of all. She has jilted me for another guy. She is going out with Ankush. I don't know what she sees in him. He is such a wimp. He just isn't good enough for her.

I even tried telling her that. In fact, I called her up the minute I found out about their movie plans. But she didn't even hear me out. She hung up on me before I could begin. I called her several times after that but her phone was busy. I guess she put the receiver off the hook.

Why is she giving me the cold shoulder? She knows I have her best interests at heart. How could I not? This is no puppy love or some crazy infatuation. This is it. The real thing. She is the one. I have told her this over and over.

Why can't she hear the voice of my heart? Why can't she take me seriously? She knows I would do anything for her. When we went to Kulu Manali on that college trip last year and she fell sick, I was there by her side. When she went to Kanpur for a wedding last year and a sudden curfew was imposed, I was there. Whenever she needed me, I was there. Yet, she has never been grateful. In any case, it's not her gratitude that I want. All I want is her love—the only thing she is not willing to give me. What is a guy supposed to do?

It all started well. We went from being neighbours to friends. For one whole month, we had a good thing going. And then? Well, I could have sworn she wanted more. I certainly did! She gave me all these signs: flashed that special smile each time I waved at her from my balcony, called me a couple of times a week, let me borrow her notes. I thought we were both ready to take our relationship to the next level. But when I suggested as much, she just shut me out. I don't know if it was something I said or didn't. But whatever it was, she just threw me out of her life. Forever. That was one year ago.

And here I am, still living in hope. In the hope that someday she will realize the folly of her actions, that she will see we are meant to be, that she will take me back. Then I hear that she is going out with this jerk, Ankush. I don't know what to do. Should I call up and threaten him or something? But he won't take a crank-caller seriously. Besides, I am not a coward. I want to say it to his face, 'Lay off! Don't you dare look at her. She is mine.'

I wonder if I should ask my friends for advice. Bad idea! They did know about us, but that was a long time ago. Public memory is short, and people can be amazingly selfish about things that don't concern them. My friends, for instance, keep telling me to 'let go', 'get over it', that I 'will get someone much better'. Right! As if they would listen to me and give up on the love of their lives.

Anyway, there was a TV show I watched where the guy loved his girl so dearly that he waited for her all his life. She went ahead, married another guy, had two children and, when her husband died, she renewed her correspondence with this dork. They finally got together when they were like seventy.

I certainly don't want to wait for the next fifty years. Aren't the college years supposed to be 'the best years of my life'? So obviously, I want to be out there celebrating our love now. How will we go on dates when we won't even have teeth? And how will we go for long walks in the moonlight when we'll need to use walking sticks to go from the bedroom to the bathroom.

No, I had to do something. And fast.

Yes, I would go to the movie theatre and tell the jerk that he was coming in the way of true love. I am sure she has kept him in the dark about me. Not that there is much to hide. But you know how girls are. They like to make such a big deal of small things. The last time we spoke, for instance, her face was black as thunder. She had snatched her hand away from me. Gosh, don't remind me of her hand. It was like butter. So soft, so smooth, and her pale skin contrasting with my dark skin. I didn't want to bathe for days. I kept looking at the hand that was consecrated by her touch.

Coming back to my story, that last time she had slapped my hand away, she had slapped it a little too hard. I had never seen her so angry. There was pure disgust on her face. How I wished I could replace that look with her thousand watt smile. Anyway folks, I am sure she will smile at me like that today. When I save her from that lump of lard, Ankush.

Okay, so here I am, at the theatre. There they are. She is alighting from the car. He is respectfully holding the door open. I step up. There is sheer terror on her face. 'Y-y-you,' she splutters. The tone of voice hurts me more than anything she could have said. She sounds like she hates me. 'Dial 101, dial 101,' she tells Ankush.

He looks flabbergasted. 'Call the cops, Ankush, now! He is not supposed to be here. Or anywhere close to me. 100 yards, at least a 100 yards, the judge had told this s-s-stalker,' she literally spits the words out.

I have tears in my eyes. She still hasn't forgiven me for training that telescope on her room. I can see that. I guess I shouldn't have told her about the telescope. It just slipped out of my mouth one day. That was the day she stopped talking to me.

'Ruma…Listen,' I try to explain but she will have none of it. 'How dare you, you sick freak! How dare you come back to ruin my life! Go away! Get lost!' She is screaming her lungs out. A crowd is collecting around us. I see a traffic cop coming towards us and I do the only thing I can. Run.

Well-placed

AHMED FAIYAZ

'Please remain silent! You are creating a lot of commotion. In a few minutes, Mr Mayur Sachdeva, General Manager of Mitsteel in India, and Ms Preeti Kumar, HR Manager of the proposed plant and an alumnus of the 2004 batch, will be on the campus,' I said, while the whole lot of them turned their attention towards me and glared at me with anxiety.

It was Day Zero, one of the most important days in the life of an MBA student at B. Y. Shah School of Business. We had been ranked among the top fifteen business schools in India and the second best school in Mumbai based on the SPG-Longhorn and Business Hindustan survey. Predictably, many blue chip companies and big names in banking and media were lining up for a slot to recruit the B. Y. Shah bred young guns with the intention to groom them as the architects of their future success. Or maybe they were just out to do what everyone else was—recruit mostly overpaid, arrogant and over-confident kids from premier business schools.

Mitsteel was the first company on campus on Day Zero. Or so they believed. In fact, they were the fifth company on campus as we had a Day Minus-One, you see. I was coordinating the placement process with two other volunteers from my batch, Rishi and Manoj, who had the honour of showing the recruiters to the restroom, serving tea, coffee and biscuits, bringing flowers and ordering lunch.

I walked up to my boyfriend Anuj Saxena, the placement committee head, who was applying for the job.

'All the very best Anuj, I know you'll do it. It will be great for us if you land an offer with Mitsteel,' I said, giving him a hug, knowing that getting this job would brighten my future prospects.

'I'm really nervous. Tell me about this company and the recruiters. What do we know about them? What are they offering exactly?' *Yes, this is what he was really interested in.*

'Mitsteel is offering 60,000 dollars per annum for a position in human resources. They recently struck a deal with the government to invest over five hundred million dollars in a Greenfield facility which reportedly has huge iron ore deposits.' Anuj nodded his head with interest. The salary package certainly excited him.

'Impress Preeti; she was a member of the placement committee while in college and played an important role in bringing Mitsteel down to campus. Okay, they are already here! I have to run... All the best!'

I ran up to Ms Preeti Kumar who had just walked in.

'Good morning, Ma'am. I hope your stay at Supreme Residences was good that and you had a comfortable ride from the hotel.' I put on my best fake smile trying to make her feel important. Truth be told, I didn't care how her stay was. I myself had barely slept, organizing the placement week.

'Yes, it was okay, thanks. Please give me the list for the two group discussions. I hope everyone is ready,' she said sharply. She seemed like a tough nut to crack.

'Yes, they are, Ma'am. I just wanted to say how much I am in awe of you and how proud we are to have you as an alumnus. Zaira at Prudential Capital, who is my mentor and your former batch mate, holds you in high regard and as an example of success for people like us.' *Like I care what she thinks, to be honest.*

'Oh, she did, did she? That's kind of her. I must call her sometime,' she replied, giving me a broad smile.

I continued regardless. 'I have marked out some of the students who have shown a lot of enthusiasm and are the pick of the batch. I just thought it would become easier for you to pick from the best and filter out those who aren't quite up to it.'

She gazed at me, narrowing her eyes a little and biting her lower lip. 'Thanks, that's good of you! Now send them in,' she said before turning around and walking away, making a clip-clop sound with her high heels. She wore a snazzy black business suit and a diamond pendant with a matching bracelet. Though she had put on some weight compared to her college days, she seemed to carry off the extra weight with elegance and managed to catch the fancy of the boys on campus. She had recently divorced her husband of three years, Mr Vinay Chugh, a former alumnus and now a Brand Manager at Crazy Cola.

I had Anuj's name on the list of the write-off candidates and all the tough contenders on the other list. They would hopefully go to war trying to eliminate each other. I marked Anuj's name along with the name of Prateek Mohanty. I didn't know who he was and how he got shortlisted. Anuj said that he didn't have a chance at the interview given his poor command over the Queen's English.

On the other list, among the strong contenders, I had marked Amarpreet Singh, who had already accepted an international offer from the Bank of Oslo. He nevertheless had to go through the process as Mitsteel were to be kept in the dark on any offers that had been made. Amarpreet was told to go and remain silent and smile through the group discussion, which would strike him out. I also marked out Tanuja Banerjee, the biggest misfit in the senior HR batch, who simply couldn't get along with anyone in class or her roommates at the hostel. If Preeti followed my lead, Anuj was in a good position to land a plum offer.

Forty-five minutes later, Preeti came out and asked Rishi to get her a strong cup of coffee. Before he left, he asked Mr Sachdeva if he needed anything.

'Sir, can I get you something? Tea, coffee, snacks…'

'Get me a large chicken supreme pizza from Pizza Palace,' he said with a scowl, running his hand over his bald pate, possibly imagining he still had hair on his head.

'Sir, I'm afraid Pizza Palace is shut as it is 10 am. I will order your pizza once it opens. Meanwhile, is there something else I can get you, sir?'

'Get me a few samosas, maybe a couple of packets of chips and cookies. Boss, get some cola too,' he ordered in a gruff voice. He sounded like a man waiting for a bypass surgery, considering he had trouble getting in through the door and took the elevator to the first floor.

Mr Sachdeva was known to be a fixer in business circles and a slick operator. He had the connections necessary to grease wheels and get things moving. Preeti clearly seemed uncomfortable around him and got on her phone at every opportunity when they were left alone. She had called me a week before they came, requesting that they be put up in rooms on separate floors.

I waited for Preeti to finish her phone call. 'How did the group discussion go? I hope you found the students enthusiastic and intelligent…'

'Oh God! That girl whose name you marked, some Banerjee, I forgot her first name but I won't forget her. She almost got up and slapped some other student who argued with her and cut her off. I must have a word with your Dean about this behaviour. They are a piece of work, really. Anyway, here's the list for the final interviews. Please get them in quickly. I want to finish this and leave,' she said icily.

'Sorry Ma'am, I guess the students got carried away in the group discussions. Yours is the first company on campus and they are very competitive. I will take this up and take care of it. I will send the shortlisted students in right away.' I walked away towards the room where all the candidates were seated. They were arguing among themselves about who did not give whom a chance to speak and how badly the entire thing went. Seeing me walk in, all of them stopped their chatter and stared with anticipation at the piece of paper in my hand.

Ranjeet, a hot-headed senior who was in the second group discussion, took my arm and pulled me aside.

'I am extremely irritated. I will go in and confront that pig-faced bald moron! I'm not worried what happens to me after that,' he said with an agitated look on his face.

'Calm down and tell me what happened.' I tried to calm his nerves, in a bid to avoid a fiasco of any kind.

'The loser just sat there and stared inappropriately at Smita throughout the group discussion. He paid no attention to what anyone was saying. I'll knock his teeth out.'

'Relax, why do you want to spoil your future? These are big shots, let it pass.'

'Ranjeet, come and sit down, there is no need to spill blood over something stupid. So what if he was looking at me? Please stop overreacting,' Smita said. Ranjeet turned around and walked back timidly to the bench where Smita sat like a queen with folded arms.

Smita was popularly called the dumb blonde of our batch. We guessed she believed it to be a compliment since, in addition to having little between her ears, she actually went and got her hair dyed blonde! Ankit, a senior, made fun of her in a couple of blogs a few months ago and managed to end up with a black eye. It was like she went out with Ranjeet for protection. The guys in college found her gorgeous and swooned over her.

'Amarpreet, Smita, Suhas, Prateek and Anuj have made it to the final round. The rest of you, all the very best for your next process, whenever that maybe. Now please clear out while we let those in the final round prepare for the interview,' I said authoritatively.

Most of the students were livid on hearing the list of names that had been announced. These were some of the comments I managed to catch,

'Amarpreet! What's so great about that guy? Saala, B.Comm. graduate from Sherwood College! He's already got one offer and he's been shortlisted by Mitsteel too. Don't they realise I went to IIT…'

'That Amarpreet didn't open his mouth. That's my strategy in my next few group discussions. Yes, that's how you do it! Allow people to attack each other and sit quietly playing the nice guy.'

'Smita? How on earth did she make it? The group discussion was about global warming and she was talking about SARS. It is really surprising, man! That joker Prateek, how is he on the list? How did he get into this college? He's a disgrace…'

'I agree. All the people who spoke very little or spoke rubbish are on that list. Except, Suhas—he's the only one who said something sensible. I hope he makes it and not that politician Anuj.'

I had had enough of the comments and walked up to Amarpreet, who looked like he was having fun.

'Okay, Amarpreet. Go in, you're first on this list. Remember you've got to tank this. We cannot have you getting two offers as we cannot disappoint either of these recruiters.'

'Yes, yes, don't worry dear. I'll take care of it,' he said with a mischievous grin. He was one of the most likeable seniors in the batch. I went back to the room and spent some time encouraging Anuj and motivating him. I got back a few minutes later as Preeti had requested and managed to peep in and catch the last few minutes of Amarpreet's interview.

'So what are your long term career goals, Amarpreet? Where do you see yourself in the next five years?' Preeti asked, gazing at him intently, trying to read his thoughts.

'I hope to see myself on the stage. You see, I am a theatre actor and I love acting. After working with your company for a few years I can save up enough to take up acting on stage full time.' He smiled innocently and Mr Sachdeva glared at him like a bear woken from his sleep. Preeti looked disappointed. He had seemed like the most likeable of the lot.

'Why did you apply for this job then?' Mr Sachdeva asked gruffly.

'You see, sir, my father also works for a steel plant. I grew up in Jamshedpur which has many steel plants,' Amarpreet explained with a straight face.

'If you had to tell us not to take one person, who would that be? Which of the five we have shortlisted? Also tell us why,' Preeti asked before Amarpreet could go on any further.

'I wouldn't pick myself, given my long-term ambitions. But the rest of them are good.'

'Thanks for being honest, you can go. Please send Suhas in,' Preeti said, noticing me at the door.

While Suhas was inside, Anuj grilled Amarpreet on the questions he was asked and the answers he gave them, while Prateek stood around with a dumb look on his face. Smita sat back without a care in the world, munching on biscuits and sipping juice that Ranjeet had brought for her.

Anuj called Prateek and Smita aside for a chat. 'They are asking who you will not pick among the rest of us. Suhas is in there and he is definitely going to say one of our names. Tell them he is not a team player, or his interests lie in marketing. And Smita, maybe you could talk about how he behaved with you.' Both of them looked at him unconvinced and unsure of what to say. 'Just do it, if you want the job.'

'I'll name these two instead. That way it won't be obvious,' he said to me later with a wicked grin. 'Now go and see what that Suhas is telling them.'

I managed to catch the last bit of his interview.

'Sir, joining Mitsteel is my dream job. I would not pick Anuj as all he's done in the past two years is to play politics. He has not done any assignments but has managed to attach his name to the group that gets the highest marks. You will see him come in here and put down others who deserve to be picked,' he said convincingly.

'Thank you Suhas, that was interesting. We'll be in touch,' Preeti said with a flirtatious smile. Suhas was quite popular among the girls.

Smita walked in next and I managed to step in and stand by the door at the end of her interview. Her interview went on the longest as Mr Sachdeva seemed to be asking her about how many people were in her family, their career choices, who lives where and other such nonsensical questions.

'Sir, I wouldn't pick Suhas as he isn't a team player. Also, he does not know how to treat women nicely. I have had a bad experience with him,' she said looking upset.

She walked out a minute later with a haughty air about herself and began texting furiously on her phone. Noticing her confidence Anuj felt insecure and I had to take him aside. 'Don't worry. She vented her anger out on Suhas. He made a big mistake by getting her pregnant.' Suhas was Smita's first boyfriend in college. Soon after her abortion and getting dumped by him, she latched on to Ranjeet.

I stood by the door to overhear what Prateek was saying. His interview lasted less than five minutes and I missed most of what went down. Apparently, this is what was said.

'Sir, I would not pick Suhas, he isn't a team player and he is more interested in a marketing job. Actually, I'm not sure. This is what Anuj requested us to say, to be honest. I feel you should not take Amarpreet as he already has accepted an offer with the Bank of Oslo.'

I walked in soon after his interview and saw Mr Sachdeva and Preeti fuming at me. 'Please send Anuj in and do ask your Dean to come and see us,' she snapped, gritting her teeth.

While I went and intimated our dean, who was busy reading the *Mid-Day*, Anuj was getting grilled about being the college politician. I saw Anuj come out from the room sweating and he rushed towards the restroom. I stood by the door to catch what was going on.

'Anuj is a big risk and I wouldn't bet on him. A lot of what he said doesn't add up. He hasn't done much but play campus politics,' Preeti said and added, 'Suhas, on the other hand...'

'I wouldn't pick Suhas either. He is an indecent fellow! My pick is Prateek. He is quiet and rustic in his ways and this is useful considering where the plant is being set up. He will be a natural fit. Plus, I promised Ojha, the MLA of Jugaadpur, that we will give his nephew a job,' Sachdeva said tactfully.

'Also give an offer letter to Smita, she will be my Executive Assistant,' he said with a wolfish grin.

'Okay,' she said reluctantly, knowing he had the final word.

The Dean stood behind me, ready to go in and get shot down for making them believe that they were first on campus.

What happened after this, you might ask.

Well, I did see Preeti talking to Suhas before she left. Later that night, she took him for dinner to give him career advice. Mr Sachdeva asked Smita to meet him at his hotel to discuss her role and responsibilities in detail. She and Ranjeet fought afterwards and broke up over her decision to join Mitsteel. Prateek and I spent the night together to celebrate his job offer at Mitsteel. I quit the placement committee and took off with him to Goa for a holiday.

The Café with No Name

SNEH THAKUR

This was Dinshaw's favourite part of the day.

For over fifty years, at the break of dawn in the city by the sea, Dinshaw walked down the pebbled street by the Parsi Colony. He loved the quietness of these mornings; it was only in the wee hours of the mornings that the city bore some resemblance to the city he grew up in. Now pushing 72, Dinshaw liked counting the rare white pebbles on the street on his way to the café he ran near H. H. College. Passed down through generations of his family, the café was equally legendary for its 'double cheese omelettes' and 'bun maska' as it was for its location near one of the finest colleges in Mumbai. The city around him had changed. Skyscrapers, bustling traffic, billboards, more traffic, but this little café with no name stood stubbornly. The old walls now bore cracks and the yellow peeling paint revealed the last coat of white paint inside like a peek into its old soul.

Even at 72, Dinshaw was a man of habit. His mornings started early with a walk towards the café at 5 a.m. He always stopped by the little boy at the corner of the street for his subsidized copy of the daily newspaper. In a small packet under his arm, he would carry the remains of last night's dinner for the dogs near the café, who would eagerly await his arrival with wagging tails. He would knock on the tin sheet door of his café with his cane, as though to announce his arrival and with Jhumka, his help for over fifteen years, they would open the doors to yet another delicious day.

Generations of students had sat on the little black chairs of the café. These chairs, Dinshaw always liked to boast, were imported for 2 rupees from Belgium back in the day. The students always humoured the old man with the stoop and big glasses which made his eyes look larger than life. Even though the canteens around the café had moved on to include the latest in snacking food, like foreign sounding sandwiches, Dinshaw had stayed true to the character of the food served at his café. In the early traffic of the mornings, you would always find endless cups of steaming chai, golden bronzed cheese omelettes and the legendary bun maska, smothered with butter and crisped to perfection, being served to the crammed café. It is ironic now to think that, not too long back, the café had almost gone out of business with the avian flu scare. But the college, the lifeline of the café, had soon brought life back into its weary walls and to Dinshaw's home, which he had built from the money earned at the café.

Like the leaves that changed colour from green to golden outside the café, times had changed. Where once the early morning traffic of students included the earnest studious types, Dinshaw now opened his doors to boys and girls in t-shirts and jeans waiting on bikes. The 'BPO employees' they called themselves, who worked through the night and went home in the mornings. Dinshaw often wondered how parents allowed their kids to work like that. In his time, an honest day's work always meant leaving home at 6 a.m. and returning home in the evening to your wife and kids. Kids who had now left home to study and work in America, and his darling Zeenah who had passed away a decade ago. In his private thoughts, Dinshaw was thankful for the café. He was thankful for the diversion it gave him from his loneliness and solitude. Here, on his seat by the cash counter, he could watch the lives of others as they laughed, ate and fought. And for this, he was thankful.

The waiters, Ravi and Jai Kishen, did not like Dinshaw. To them, he was the overbearing boss who was always watching them from his counter, making sure that exact servings of butter were being handed out with the toasts, and that the money for each cup of chai was accounted for properly.

'*Oye Jai! Ek scrambled egg, jaldi!*' Scrambled eggs.

Amit liked scrambled eggs. Dinshaw remembered the boy who used to sit alone in the corner of the café. Always scribbling in his blue notebook, as though he had to catch the flight of every thought that passed through his head. He came every evening from H. H. College after his classes. His order was always the same—one chai and one plate of scrambled eggs. No matter how hurriedly the boys would serve him the food, Amit sat in that corner for hours till the eggs turned soggy and the chai cold. At closing time, he would quickly glug the chai down and ask for the eggs to be parcelled. On his way out, he would smile at Dinshaw and ask him about his wellbeing. For years, Dinshaw had sat at the very same counter, handing out the remaining bill change to the students that came there, but no one ever spoke to Dinshaw. For most, he was just the same old Parsi Bawa, always dressed in white and black, who wore a stern expression on his face. But Amit was different; he always noticed little things and complimented Dinshaw on them: like the marble tops on the tables which were always sparkly clean or the fact that the bun maska, even though smothered with butter, cost only 4 rupees while the shop across the road sold butter sandwiches for ₹10. It was these little things that made Dinshaw break his rule of never befriending a customer.

Amit was the son of a tyre dealer in Gwalior. His was a small family—a mother who taught at the local primary school, and a sister who was studying in the 12th grade. Times had turned tough at home when his father's business was suddenly ridden with debt from customers who had not paid up, and the company whose credit period had run its course. Yet, his father had made sure that Amit made it to the finest college in Mumbai. With two thousand rupees, a hold-all with beddings and a tin trunk containing a few pairs of clothes and black shoes, Amit had landed in Mumbai. He lived in a dormitory near the college which had rows of beds and a common bathroom at the end of the dorm. Every morning, there would be a queue outside the baths. The boys would call out numbers to 'book' their turn in the bath. To save time and make it to college at the right hour, Amit would bathe in the middle of the night. He would wash his clothes and keep them in a bucket close to his bed and dry them in the morning on the thin wire outside his window. At college, he would work hard to keep up. An ordinary student, he was amazed by the intelligence of the city kids. Hours of tutoring after college hours had made them proficient in the theorems and sciences which he struggled with. With no money to fund the 'private lessons' that his professors gave after college hours, he sat at the café near college writing down theorem after theorem in an effort to etch them into his memory.

On many evenings, Dinshaw would send another steaming cup of chai over to Amit, sometimes even a well-buttered bun maska. Having a reputation of being frugal, the waiters Ravi and Jai Kishen found this sudden generosity odd, gossiping amongst themselves behind kitchen doors. Amit would shy away from accepting anything without paying, but Dinshaw insisted. Dinshaw had understood that Amit had little money to get by each month and that the scrambled eggs at his café were Amit's dinner. He found Amit's honesty endearing. It reminded him of the time when he was younger, when he would save a sliver of chocolate from his lunch hour for dinner, even though his Zeenah found this ridiculous.

'What Deenshaw, we have enough a!' she would say and Dinshaw would lovingly look at her and say, 'What if the kids wanted more? At least, now, I have a secret treat tucked away!'

As days went by, an unusual friendship evolved between Amit and Dinshaw. On weekends, Amit would come in a bit early. He would carry the most recent novel he had borrowed from the college library. He would show Dinshaw the cover and summarize the story so far. Together, they would talk about books, Mumbai and Dinshaw's favourite pieces of classical music. Dinshaw let Amit borrow his old LPs. It was Dinshaw who introduced Amit to the world of opera and jazz. After big wins in cricket matches, Amit would detail the game to Dinshaw over a cup of steaming chai, telling him about the catches and the misses. Dinshaw opened the doors of his café each day looking forward to meeting Amit. Talking to Amit, he felt younger, cared for and more alive. Amit had become Dinshaw's window to the world.

'The *internet* Dinshaw Baba, it's called the *internet*,' Amit would inform Dinshaw.

'So it is true, Ameet? This thing which sends letters in one second with no stamp?'

Amit smiled. These conversations often amazed him. How much the world had changed in just a decade! He would often relay these talks to his friends at college, who found them humorous. Amit just found these conversations insightful of the little world in which Dinshaw lived, surrounded by aged, yellow-paged letters, old LPs and postage stamps, licked and pasted as though mailing a part of the sender through a letter, many miles way.

The day Amit graduated, Dinshaw let everyone in the café have an extra knob of butter with their toast. He was as proud as a father could be of the boy who sat in his café and was now heading out to face the world. He told Amit to take up a respectable job and make sure to send his father 75 per cent of the money he earned.

'Ameet, my boy,' he said. 'You are a young man now. The world is your oyster, but never forget the family who gave you so much.'

'Or you, Baba, for all those free chais and scrambled eggs na?' Amit replied with a mischievous twinkle in his eye.

'No boy, you are like my own son,' said Dinshaw. Two magnified tears welled up behind his glasses, which he promptly wiped away with his sleeve.

Amit did find a respectable job at Digiworld Technologies. While the pay was lesser than what any of his batch mates were getting from other employers, it gave him a chance to learn new skills such as negotiation and sales. Amit did not like this very much and over weekends, when he visited the café, he often complained to Dinshaw.

'Did I study for this, Baba? To hang like a monkey on trains all day, smelling other people's armpits! And even then, Mr Ghosh is not happy... He thinks I lack commitment!'

Dinshaw called for another plate of scrambled eggs and calmly explained to Amit how, even when he thought the café was not for him, he learnt that a profession was different from a hobby. Amit did not like Dinshaw's reasoning in these matters, but did not want to hurt the old man's feelings. Instead, he took another heaped spoonful and stared out at the happy faces around, wishing. He wished that he was Vikram, his batch mate and the son of a wealthy industrialist who didn't have to bother about grades or a job because his dad had 'taken care' of all of that for him. He wished he had a fancy car and a mobile phone, both of which seemed attainable in the big dreams he had spun sitting in his college classroom. The future had seemed so promising then. Now, sitting in the same cafe as he had for over two years, he felt despondent, as though everything was a waste. As though all those memorized theorems and cheated-on tests had become life-sized creatures forming a net around him, in which he was trapped forever.

'Ameet, you need to be stronger than this, boy. It happens. It is life. Keep going. It will all be fine.' Dinshaw threw his arm around Amit's shoulder and patted him reassuringly. 'I too went through many ups and downs, when I took over this cafe, when Zeenah died, when my children moved away...It all will settle. You are just being impatient, boy.'

'Impatient?' Amit snapped. 'Impatient? Well maybe I did not have a "family business" to bail me out and that is why I am "impatient"...What would *you* know? You were handed a running café, na?'

Dinshaw gasped. He felt as though the café had suddenly fallen into a vacuum with no air left to breathe.

'Okay beta, don't worry,' Dinshaw managed to say with much difficulty. 'Here, take this chai.' Dinshaw handed over the cup to Amit, trying unfruitfully to keep his shaking hands steady, given away by the soft tremor of the shaking cup and saucer.

Following the incident at the café, a sort of quiet distance had formed between Dinshaw and Amit. Amit was regretful of having blurted those words, having said them in a fit of annoyance, but he found it difficult to apologize to Dinshaw. He tried to make up for his guilt by continuing to visit Dinshaw, but the camaraderie was lost, as though suspended in the air somewhere in the café, out of reach to both of them.

Days turned into weeks, and weeks into months and Amit had turned into a distant memory. Dinshaw would get a phone call now and then. Amit was promoted, his new girlfriend was called Mansi, he bought a second-hand bike, and he went home and got his sister engaged. Dinshaw gave Amit his blessings each time. But somewhere deep inside, he felt cheated, as though someone had been sneaking food out of his café or handing out an extra knob of butter without his knowledge. Ravi and Jai Kishen bore the brunt of Dinshaw's bad moods. Dinshaw would lose his cool frequently, sometimes screaming across the crowded café to scold them about a chipped cup or an unclean plate. It seemed to them like a gloomy cloud had descended around the clear Mumbai skies and refused to leave.

Dinshaw had changed, but life around the café remained the same. The clatter of the plates, steaming whiffs of tea, crunches of crisp toasts, the soft din of conversations around projects, strict professors and college beauties continued. The business continued to open its doors to the 'BPO kids' and a new semester had started in the college, making evenings interesting with 'introduction' sessions between seniors and freshers outside the café, where intimidated freshers tried their hand at singing and proposing to people they had just met.

It would have been just another ordinary day if it weren't for the faint thump of an Enfield bike which got louder as it got closer. The dust on the road rose gently as if to greet its visitor, the clanging sounds at the café drowned in the sounds of the bike. The students turned curiously to see who it was. A glimpse of a flying red scarf and a biker helmet. Dinshaw adjusted his glasses and looked up. A familiar face smiled back at him.

'Dinshaw Baba. This…is Mansi.'

The skies were sunny again.

Between Friends

PARITOSH UTTAM

There was desolation all around
until you became my friend
the best companion I ever found
on the journey to life's end

said the Hallmark card. Mushy, sing song, pretentious.

For someone who brings Hope to Life,
For someone who stands by us till Eternity,
For someone who is a True Friend

said the Archies one. Impersonal, clichéd, too many capitals.

Siddhartha moved out of the greeting cards section and saw the little heart-shaped plaque of red velvet with silver lettering across it: *I found a friend in you.* He got it gift-wrapped and taped a card on it addressed to 'Dear Sanjana'.

Dear Sanjana, as expected, was sitting alone at the table at the farthest end from the entrance to the cafeteria. The cafeteria was one place in the Pune University campus that was never empty, unlike the college library or the gymkhana, until it closed late in the night. Siddhartha strode up to her table, pulled up a chair and sat facing her.

'Knew you would be here.'

'Where else you know you can always find me here.' She spoke with the same lack of punctuation that she practised in her emails. She did not seem surprised by his arrival. Her voice, husky, sounded as though she suffered from a perennial sore throat. But it went along with the rest of her appearance, as if The Maker, in giving her a masculine frame, wanted to go the whole stretch. Indeed, if she had a soft, girlish voice, it would have been all the more incongruous.

'Well, happy birthday,' Siddhartha said, holding out his hand to shake hers. She accepted his wishes, again without showing any surprise at his remembering, although he could see she was pleased. He then took out the gift-wrapped box from his pocket, rearranged the card and placed it before her. This evoked some reaction.

'Oh wow thanks can I open it here.' The wrapper was in her hands before he could reply.

'Thanks Sid it is sweet,' she said, holding the plaque in her hand. He knew she meant it and felt pleased because she was.

He looked at the tables behind him, worried that someone might be watching them. From a distance, one would see only a red heart and not the wording on it, and the implication could be embarrassing. Siddhartha let out a silent sigh of relief as, thankfully, no one was looking their way.

Would he really feel embarrassed if the campus grapevine carried rumours linking Sanjana and him romantically? Perhaps not. Rather, it would be funny. Of all the girls in the college, his friends would mock, Sid could not find anybody other than Sanju baba. But she had a heart of gold. What had happened with Ankita? Barbie doll-like plastic beauty, and with as much plastic in her heart. She had not wasted much time in moving on to Akshay, only because his father was rich enough to gift him his own car. Siddhartha could not imagine her losing any sleep over ditching him. Her last words to him, weeks ago, had been, 'Let's remain friends, Sid?' Of course there was no inverse relation between a girl's beauty and nature, but one example of either case in one's life—Ankita, beautiful but cruel, Sanjana, plain but kind-hearted— went a long way in establishing a hypothesis.

Sanjana sat hunched forward, elbows resting on the table, blowing and creating a mini-whirlpool in the cup of coffee between them. The arms of her denim jacket were folded back at the cuffs, revealing wrists a tennis player would have been proud of. Her hair barely reached her shoulders, and at the front they hung straight down like the frayed edge of a curtain, framing her face. Siddhartha saw with a start that something in her face had altered. The eyebrows. She had got them shaped, apparently deciding that they did not have to be thick, bushy ones that met over the bridge of her nose.

Siddhartha decided that it would take much more than eyebrow-shaping to make her look good, or he had simply gotten used to her earlier appearance. But he was touched, for never before had she shown the slightest concern about her looks, and now it seemed as if the woman in her had, at last, decided to wake up from dormancy.

'Something on your mind what are you thinking,' she asked.

'Nothing,' he said quickly, laughing to himself. That was Sanjana—sometimes he feared she could read his thoughts when he thought she was not even looking.

'Is it Ankita when will you forget her?'

'No, no. Long time since I thought of her.'

'Good.'

She had got it wrong this time. He was not thinking of Ankita at all. What he said was true, well almost true, because one never gets over a first love, especially when it fails. But it had stopped hurting now, and that was what Sanjana wanted to hear.

The tears and the pangs of sorrow and anger were very much

there—before he met Sanjana. Despite being sympathetic, none of his friends were able to comfort him. A pat on the back with the words, 'It happens to everyone, dude. Move on,' were indicative of their support but did not provide solace. And a 20-year-old guy in college cannot weep on the shoulders of other 20-year-old guys.

One needs feminine shoulders for that, and the broad ones of Sanjana, though no less masculine in appearance, had come to his aid. He remembered quite clearly, soon after his break-up, coming to the cafeteria for lunch alone, unable to join in the usual banter of his classmates, discussing movies and cricket matches. He did not want to be a damp squib in their conversation. The only vacant table was Sanjana's. Shrugging his shoulders, he sat opposite her and ate in silence, a blank stare fixed on his plate.

'Forget her she is not worth it.' The rapid-fire sentence coming from Sanjana, still bent over her plate, startled him. He began to get angry but then imagined the despondent and ridiculous figure he must be making, so obvious to all, that he had to laugh. She looked up with an impish smile and their friendship took off from there.

Their meeting in the cafeteria at lunch and teatime became regular. She was in a different class, so they did not meet in the same lectures, but he soon found himself looking forward to their meetings in the cafeteria. At first he was teased: 'Of all the girls, Sanju baba!' The unkind name, alluding to the macho Bollywood hero Sanjay Dutt, was not without basis. He could not deny her manly girth, her slouching gait and the fact that she was the only girl in college who rode a geared bike, a 150 cc one at that, without even resorting to the electronic start.

After a while, it stopped mattering. And when his friends saw him recovering his earlier cheerfulness and humour, they refrained from teasing him. Sanjana was refreshingly different from the other girls he met: she talked with directness, bereft of any girlish airs or giggly behaviour, but with a sensitivity that was soothingly feminine.

His physique, slighter in comparison to hers, must have made them seem an odd couple. The thought, coming to him while he watched her finish her coffee, surprised him. It was funny to think of themselves as a couple.

'So what's the plan tonight? Where's the birthday party?' he asked.

'No party I am here where would I go.'

'Come on! Not even tonight?'

'No you know I don't go out.'

Siddhartha snorted in exasperation. He carried on, failing to notice that her smile had become fixed. 'Don't be silly. Let's go out and have a wonderful dinner. How about Chinese? All Stir Fried at E-Square? Just next door. Expensive, I admit, but we can enjoy one day in a year, right?'

'No thanks Sid I said no.' Even the fixed smile had vanished and, this time, he didn't miss the seriousness.

'But why?'

'Because I don't go out especially with guys it gives the wrong ideas.' After a pause, unusual for her, she added, 'To others.'

He gaped at her.

'I am sorry you find me old-fashioned,' she said and shrugged, the gesture belying her feeling sorry. 'E-square dinner movie and so on.'

'But it's me!' he said. 'Not just some guy.'

'I know but...' she shrugged again. 'Sorry.'

Fury writhed inside him like a serpent. He had offered the idea of dinner out of pure friendship, and that she should misconstrue it as a cheap overture was demeaning to him. Maybe his idea was not so pure, maybe there was an element of overture in it, but that she should turn it down mortified him. Coming from her, it was as big an insult as he could imagine.

Had it been Ankita, he could have borne it. But Sanjana? The Sanjana who was so manly that the guys mocked her behind her back for never wearing anything other than jeans and shirts, the Sanjana who was so friendless that she had to eat alone— that Sanjana had turned down his harmless offer and was acting unapproachable.

Unapproachable to him, whom even Ankita had once found attractive. The wrathful serpent in his heart sat up, ready to strike and spit venom.

'But it's all right to meet here daily? That doesn't give wrong ideas to others?'

Sanjana frowned. 'You crazy or what.'

'Oh yes I am crazy. Meeting here is fine, but going out is wrong. Shaping your eyebrows and waiting for me here, that doesn't give wrong ideas?'

She stared at him. A tear glistened briefly and vanished as suddenly as it had appeared. Her face hardened and smoothed out the creases in her forehead. She got up.

'Look, I didn't mean that,' he began, but she had already pushed her chair back so hard that it fell over with a crash. He could only watch her back receding away from him on the way out.

Outside, a motorbike burst into life and roared away.

Siddhartha set the chair back upright and finished his coffee. Then he too got up and went out slowly. The road was empty. To one side, on the top of a garbage pile, a shiny red plaque caught his eye. He kicked the rubbish over it until it was lost to sight.

Dimples and Cute Smiles

RANJANI MUTHU

Paedodontics (Paediatric Dentistry) is something I have always been wary of. Kids are noisy, they refuse to listen, bawl into your ears, kick and thrash about, and often bite as well. No, I don't fancy paedodontic work at all. To cajole, coax by sweet-talk and struggle with them is way too much time and energy expended.

In fact, a paedodontic appointment normally takes twice the time and ten times the energy than one with an adult patient. The child first needs to be made to just sit by himself on the dental chair. This is easier said than done. For convenience, let us assume that the 'child' is a boy in this example. Next, four pairs of hands grab his head, hands and legs. If he still does not cooperate, the parent is asked to sit on the chair and hold the child. Then, five pairs of hands clamp the child and force him into submission until the dentist completes his job. One would think this was a perfectly safe straitjacket but, despite so many restraints, I have been kicked, bitten, *and* scratched!

With the child moving all the parts of his body in different directions at breakneck speed, the dentist has to aim and either inject or use the drill in that limited area. This is akin to trying to thread a needle while doing an energetic dance number. To be able to do it successfully, dentists deserve an additional degree! (Nowadays, with the availability of sedation, this scenario is thankfully becoming a rarity.)

I still remember my first paedodontia posting in the National Dental College, Chennai. It was in May '81, an experience I will not forget any time soon. After two years of pre-clinical work—working on models (called phantom heads, which are replicas of the head and mouth)—we were posted in clinics, where we were to handle patients. There is a world of a difference between the two. Models can be manipulated any way you want, are totally compliant and, above all, don't bite!

Students were divided into batches and were posted in the different departments of Dentistry. The moment we heard our first clinical posting was paedodontia, my friend Anjali was excited. I was not. She 'loved' children, she said, while I would run a mile from them. Anjali always had the feeling that she could get along well with kids of all ages. She liked them. Girls were cute, but having two wildly boisterous boys for brothers had possibly led her to think she knew how to handle boys. The scruffier and the naughtier they were, the cuter they looked to her! So when I said I was dreading the posting she said, 'Don't be silly, Aditi. What on earth gave you such an idea! Kids may be difficult initially, but they are not dumb, you know. You only have to treat them right and you will have them eating out of your hands.'

Right, why didn't I think of that?

'All right, wise girl, how exactly do I treat them right?'

'Take a little time and explain what you plan to do. Ask a few questions about what they like, get them interested, and take their mind off the treatment. Then see how they cooperate!' she explained.

'You make it sound so simple,' I said.

'It is simple if you know how to handle them,' said Anjali confidently. 'What do you expect the poor things to do? The child cries not because of pain but because of the strange place and cold, unfamiliar creatures in white coats that hover about menacingly who, without warning, take a syringe and jab it into their mouth. No wonder the kid screams. I would have died in his place,' she said.

'Boy, Anjie, you seem quite the expert in child psychology,' I said in awe.

'I truly love kids. I feel they are special. You need to talk to them like you would to adults. Then see how they hang on to your every word.'

'But what can you ask a kid when you see him for the first time? You can't discuss the anatomy of the human brain with him, can you?'

'Very funny. Discuss his favourite game. If it is a girl, discuss dolls and tell her a story of a doll's house and the different kinds of clothes you can dress the dolls in. Put the kids at ease. Perhaps I just have a way with kids—I love them and they love me!' she finished with a modest laugh.

The next morning, we left for our first clinical posting, looking professional in our starched cotton saris and new white coats.

Anjali was in her I-love-kids-and-they-love-me mood and was going on about how best to approach young patients. This monologue interspersed with monosyllabic affirmations from me continued until we reached our destination. We reached the Paedodontia Department and waited for the rest of the batch to congregate there. Anjali's zeal was still in full force. And so engrossed were we in the topic that we didn't notice our batch mates listening in. When she finally stopped, we realized how everyone had been fully tuned into the discourse.

'Wow! Are you real?' they exclaimed. 'Here is someone who actually loves kids! Most of us would drop everything and run, and you say you love working with them?'

Someone said, 'Anjali, we must watch you with kids. Maybe

we'll pick up some tips on how to manage child patients.'

Anjie just smiled through all the scepticism. Once the entire batch had turned up, we stepped into the Department of Paedodontia. We could hear children screaming and yelling from all corners of the department. Everyone except Anjali had a look of dread on their faces. The Department had a small hall where ten dental chairs and a couple of benches were placed for patients to sit before and after the treatment. There was a desk with a single chair for the Assistant Professor at one corner of the room. Dr Nagaraj, a thin, wiry young man, was sitting at the Assistant Professor's desk. All of us crowded around him.

'So this is your first clinical posting? How does it feel to be able to handle patients?'

We answered in chorus, 'Great, sir!' though we didn't really feel all that great.

We spent the morning watching the kids—some screaming, some squirming, and some howling. Those lined up for fillings did cooperate, but the screamers were the ones undergoing extractions. We watched the proceedings until the outpatient hours lasted, and then broke up for tea.

While chewing on samosas the others in our batch asked Anjali, 'You claim to love kids and have a special bond with them. When do we get to see you in action?'

'Show us your magic with the kids,' some others piped in.

Anjali got her chance after a couple of weeks. We had to handle fillings before we could graduate to extractions. The day the Assistant Professor gave the green signal for extractions of shaky milk teeth, Anjali was allotted a scruffy boy, about 7 years old. I was allotted a cute little girl of five. I decided to see how Anjie managed her little fellow and follow suit. I soon realized that all the others in the batch had the same idea. As she walked past me, holding her patient's hand, she said in an undertone, 'Isn't my patient cute? Look, everyone is watching. I'll put those Doubting Thomases in their place.'

The child's mother followed them. Anjie picked up the little fellow and placed him on the chair, while the mother hovered anxiously.

Anjali asked her, 'Where's his father?'

'He is behind those doors,' said his mother. 'He is very scared of injections. See that man in the blue shirt. That's him.'

All of us turned to look at a tiny fellow in a blue checked shirt peeping through the barricades. He looked as if he would drop dead at the sight of a needle. Anjali then put on her most dazzling smile and turned to the child. The effect was devastating. The child smiled back, showing off two cute dimples. Anjali looked up and mouthed to me, 'This is going to be a breeze,' and gave me a thumbs up.

'What's your name?' she asked gaily.

'Muthu,' he replied.

'Muthu, what's the problem with your teeth?'

He pointed to the offending tooth, a mobile deciduous incisor, and said with a little finger still in his mouth, 'It hurts!'

'Don't worry, we will soon set it right,' said Anjali in her most placatory tone. Pulling out his grubby finger from his mouth, she asked, 'What games do you play, Muthu?'

'Cricket, football, running and catching...' He seemed to play a lot of games.

'Which is your favourite?'

'Cricket.'

The conversation went on along these lines for a while. Muthu said he liked to bat and bowl and, like most players, didn't like to field.

'Where do you play, Muthu?' was the next question.

'In a nearby field.'

Then Anjali asked him with an even bigger smile, 'Do you know what I am going to do to stop your pain?'

The little fellow shook his head truthfully.

Anjali explained the details.

'I am going to take a syringe and give you a tiny poke in your mouth. This will make the whole mouth numb and then with this,' she showed the forceps, 'I'll gently pull the tooth out. I promise it won't hurt one bit. And so that the injection doesn't hurt, I'm going to put some medicine.' She put a bit of lignocaine gel on some cotton and showed it to him.

'I'll apply it on the gum next to the painful tooth and then, when I give you the injection, it won't hurt at all. It will feel like a mosquito bite. You have been bitten by a mosquito, haven't you, Muthu?'

He nodded his head and put out his arm, which had a couple of reddish eruptions.

'Shall I go ahead?' she asked, to which the little boy nodded.

Anjali turned around, loaded the syringe with lignocaine and then placed it on the table.

'Okay Muthu, open your mouth.'

She put some of the lignocaine gel on another piece of cotton and applied it on the gum around the tooth and stealthily took the syringe from the table. Hand poised, just as she was about to inject, Muthu let out a ear-splitting scream. Startled, Anjali lost her footing and nearly fell and, in this commotion, poked herself in the left hand. She stifled a yelp and wiped the blood which had appeared where the needle had pricked her. Her smile lost its brilliance. She turned to Muthu.

'Now Muthu, why did you behave like that? See, I poked my hand because you screeched like that. I told you it wouldn't hurt.

Come on, you are a cricketer and so brave! Be a good boy and open your mouth.'

'I am scared,' he said in a small voice.

'Scared of what?' Anjali asked.

'Scared of the injection,' Muthu said.

Now all the interns were watching the 'drama' with renewed interest. Those who were tied up elsewhere dropped everything and came to watch the fun. With her sweetest smile well in place and a sugary tone to match, Anjali repeated what she was going to do. He nodded in agreement and a fresh syringe was taken for the task.

Muthu opened his mouth. As Anjali took a step forward a tad warily, Muthu not only screamed much louder, but started moving his head furiously from side to side. He lashed out with his hands and feet and kicked the syringe out of her hand with such force that it landed a good ten feet away. A series of lightning-fast kicks on her chest and arms made her pristine coat a sad apology for what it had been half an hour earlier.

My heart went out to Anjali. She looked like a bedraggled doll. Her hair was a mess and her coat had footprints on it which made a bizarre design. She turned to the child, now sitting quietly with an innocent smile on his face. A scowl was beginning to form on her face.

'Muthu, behave yourself or I'll...' she said gritting her teeth.

Everyone who was watching to 'learn' from Anjali was now thoroughly enjoying the carnival.

'Muthu, stop this nonsense. Open your mouth and sit still!' she commanded. She prised his mouth open and brought the syringe close, keeping her finger inside his mouth. Just then, he clamped his teeth down hard on her finger. A painful yell from Anjali echoed in the hall. The mother, aghast at Muthu's behaviour, was admonishing him and holding on to his arms, but the little monkey twisted and freed himself from her grip.

She then asked, 'Shall I ask his father to come and hold him?'

Anjali nodded, rubbing her finger where she had been bitten. The father was summoned for help and he came rushing in, unfolding his lungi, looking more petrified than helpful. The mother held on to Muthu's hands and the father was almost lying on him, holding his legs. But one look at the syringe and the child kicked this way and that, breaking free of the father. The whole scene was getting more hilarious by the minute.

By this time, Anjali was snarling and looking ready to kill. Her theories about handling children had been sent flying out the window. Two male attendants who were watching came over and told Anjali, 'This boy is not going to listen to all your smooth talk. What he needs is the two of us to hold him down. We'll hold him and you go ahead and extract. We have been watching you talk and waste everyone's time.'

Anjali bristled at the words, but she reluctantly acquiesced. All her bravado about handling the little patient on her own had disappeared. She gave me a wan smile and moved so that one attendant sat on the chair, and the other hoisted the boy on his lap and held on to his hands and legs. He then told Anjali to go ahead. Anjali took the syringe for the nth time that day and approached the child. In spite of being held by two professional nursing attendants, the child managed to squirm and move, and left Anjali dithering.

By this time, the Assistant Professor who was watching the drama had had enough. He went up to Anjali and told her he would help with the case. With the attendants still holding the child, he curtly told the parents to leave. Suddenly, the whole room fell silent. Only Muthu was screaming.

'Be quiet!' he shouted, giving the table next to him a resounding whack. Muthu's screams abruptly stopped.

There was a hushed silence. Only the ceiling fan could be heard creaking.

'Open your mouth,' he commanded.

The child quietly obliged and Anjali gave the injection. The little devil who had created such a scene sat there without a whimper. After five minutes, Anjali extracted the tooth.

Anjali made her way painfully to the medical OP to get her finger attended to and stated 'history of assault' when asked for her medical history! Later in the evening, as she was nursing her wounds, her finger and her soul, she said through gritted teeth, 'Kids! Never ever be taken in by their cute dimples and sweet smiles.'

One and One Eleven

PRATEEK GUPTA

Institute of Technology & Engineering (ITE), Jhansi
Time: Final Year (2004–05)

'My dear students,' the Dean began his announcement, 'I know you have desperately been waiting for the election results.' Calm spread out over the gathering students—this was one of the closest elections the institute had ever witnessed. 'This year, the elections were contested between two very deserving candidates. As in every election, you choose a leader and I believe that, irrespective of the election results, both the candidates will work closely for the welfare of the institute and students. This year, the two candidates in the election are Prayas Mathur & Avinash Singh. Please put your hands together for both of them.' The hall thundered with applause. 'The results for this year's election are: Avinash 496 votes and Prayas 542 votes. The president for this year is Prayas Mathur.'

Prayas stood up amidst the deafening echo of the applause. He went up to the stage and shook hands with the Dean. Through the corner of his eye, he could see Avinash and his gang leave the hall. He lost himself in the jubilation of victory and celebration and completed the ceremony with a speech filled with inspirational quotes he had copied from the Internet.

After the ceremony, Prayas picked up his bike and headed towards the central canteen. The canteen was unusually filled and he could see people from a distance. He smiled in anticipation of meeting his friends and supporters. As he inched closer to the canteen, the noises grew louder. This wasn't the usual chaos of the canteen. He stopped his bike when he saw Chotu, the canteen kid, running from the canteen.

'*Oye Chotu, kya hua, kahan bhaga jaa raha hai?*'

'*Sir, woh canteen mein bahut jhagda ho gaya hai. Bhaiya ne Warden Sir ko bula kar lane ko kaha hai.*'

'*Theek hai, jaldi bhaag kar jaa.*'

He immediately sped towards the canteen. As soon he reached, he could see the fight was between his friends and Avinash's gang. He had thought that the rivalry would be settled once and for all with the election results, but he couldn't have been more wrong.

Prayas shouted at the crowd, driving his bike inside the canteen. When Avinash's attention was diverted towards him, in a flash, a hand with a Coke bottle struck him on the back of his head. Avinash stared at him with a stoned look before falling to the ground. Initially, a thin stream of blood trickled down his ear but within no time his face was lying in a pool of blood. Prayas jumped from his bike and picked up Avinash. He took out his handkerchief and tied it over Avinash's head, which was drenched in blood. Prayas growled to one of the boys to hold Avinash and sit behind his bike while he raced towards the Medical College.

'What happened to him?' asked the doctor.

'Sir, there was a fight in the college and someone hit him with a bottle,' Prayas replied.

The doctor immediately went to inspect Avinash, who was unconscious by now. He gave some instructions to his assistant and dialled a number.

'Professor Sachan, this is Professor Bhatt from the Medical College.'

Prayas trained his ears to the doctor's voice, unable to hear the voice from the other side.

'I have a couple of students from your college. One of them is injured.' There was a pause. 'Yes, the condition is a bit critical. The injury is on the skull. We need to operate right away. You can come and sign the papers while we start operating. I will give the phone to the student who accompanied him here,' said the doctor, handing the phone over to Prayas.

'Sir, this is Prayas Mathur here.'

'Prayas! What happened? Who is injured? I got a report about a fight in canteen.'

'Sir, someone hit Avinash with a bottle and he was bleeding very heavily. So I immediately brought him to the Medical Department.'

'Is anyone else injured?'

'No sir.'

'Do you know who hit him?'

'No sir. I had just reached the canteen when I saw Avinash on the ground,' Prayas stammered.

The scene from the canteen floated in front of his eyes. He could see Avinash falling to the ground and Ravi throwing the bloodstained bottle in the corner. No matter what, he could not tell the Dean the name of the culprit. Not after all that had happened in the last four years.

'Prayas, I understand that this is a difficult time for you. But you need to understand that if Avinash is hurt, your friends may be involved. It is your duty to make sure that all the students of this institute that you represent are treated fairly. Avinash is also a student and, whether you like it or not, you are his representative too.'

'Yes sir, I understand,' Prayas meekly replied.

'Okay, I will be reaching the hospital in half an hour. You stay there and keep me informed.'

'Yes sir.'

'Also, call Sharma and ask him to keep your supporters down and out of trouble. I hope you understand the ramifications of this incident.'

'Yes sir,' Prayas replied, surrender in his tone.

The call had been disconnected without waiting for his answer. He looked up and saw that the 'Busy' sign over the operation theatre was still on. He sat in the waiting area and started thinking about the day he had met Avinash and Ravi.

♦

Institute of Technology & Engineering (ITE), Jhansi
Time: First Year (2001–02)

'Names?'

'Prayas Mathur, Avinash Singh, Ravi Sharma,' Prayas replied, freezing back to the attention position with his gaze tightly fixed on his own shoes. He had spent half an hour in the morning shining them. Now, he could see small freckles of dust settled on them.

Professor V. K. Sachan, the Dean, refocused on his computer. Prayas had heard stories about him. He was known among all the state colleges as a very strict and unforgiving administrator. It was because of him that the Government College of Engineering & Technology was the best college in the state. Prayas stole a glance across the Dean's cabin. One wall was entirely converted into a bookshelf, while the other had multiple certificates and awards he had earned in his career. He saw some books lying on the table, of which the Dean was the author.

His chain of thoughts was broken by Professor Sachan's voice.

'So you three want to share the room?'

'Yes sir,' said Prayas meekly.

'It is not possible,' he said in an indifferent tone.

Before Prayas could gather the courage to ask why, the Professor continued, 'The institute does not have any restrictions on how people share their rooms, but according to the U.P. government regulations, the first year rooms need to be based on caste—1 General candidate, 1 Schedule Caste or Schedule Tribe candidate and 1 Other Backward Classes candidate. What's your name?'

'Prayas.'

'So you cannot share a room with that Sharma. Any of you can share the room with that Singh guy. You can go now,' the Dean said with an air of finality.

Prayas thought of reasoning with him but, by then, the Dean was already occupied with his computer, ignoring his presence in the cabin.

'What happened?' Avinash asked.

'The Dean said that the three of us cannot be in the same room.'

'But why?' Ravi questioned.

'There is some rule that a room is allocated based on the caste system. Me and Ravi are both from the General category and cannot be in the same room.' He consciously avoided pointing out Avinash's caste in the discussion.

'Avinash, you choose who you want to live with. The other one will take the next room,' said Ravi.

Months later, through a series of quid pro quo arrangements, the three friends managed to end up in the same room. The exams were followed by the annual fest. This was their first taste of power, the first experience of why a college president was who he was. They had heard and seen the college president, but seeing him in action was different.

Prayas still remembered the day he had run back to the hostel to Avinash and Ravi.

'Wake up you two! You know what I just found out from Shubho Sir? Can you guess how much the budget is, which our college president controls?' Prayas asked, with excitement in his voice.

He did not wait for an answer. 'More than ₹90 lakhs! ₹50 lakhs is from the college fund and the rest of it is sponsorship.'

'Wow!' Avinash and Ravi replied in unison.

'You know what? When we are in the final year, I will be the college president,' Prayas whispered to them dreamily.

'You see the money and you want to be the president!' Ravi jibed at him.

'No man, he is so principled that he won't touch the money anyway. He only wants the post to write it on his résumé,' replied Avinash on Prayas' behalf.

'Avinash is absolutely right. I need a damn good résumé for cracking a good MBA college and this president position would look good! Money doesn't really matter,' Prayas confessed.

'You know what? We both will make sure that you will be the college president when our time comes. Right, Ravi?' asked Avinash.

'Absolutely!' said Ravi.

'Oh, it's 5 o' clock already! I have to go for those idiotic ABCW meetings,' said Avinash.

'You hate those meetings! Why do you go for every meeting?' Ravi asked.

'Every time I go, you ask me the same question when you know the answer already. Anyway, I'll join you guys in the canteen after the meeting,' Avinash replied as he left.

ABCW, the Association for Backward Class Welfare, was

basically an informal group which consisted of almost all the students and teachers from the scheduled castes, including the infamous Head of Department of Electronics. Avinash never liked those meetings because he was always condemned for being friends with the upper caste Prayas and Ravi. He forced himself to sit through the meetings as otherwise it could offend the various teachers there, leaving an impact on his internal marks.

◆

Institute of Technology & Engineering (ITE), Jhansi
Time: Second Year (2002–03)

'This institute is a crazy place!' said Ravi in an angry tone.

'Why are you so annoyed with the Insti?' Prayas asked, laughing.

'Nothing yaar, the anticipation of the result makes me jittery. You know I messed up the electronics a bit,' Ravi replied.

'Dude, where were you? I was looking for you in the hostel to call you to the canteen,' Prayas asked when he saw Avinash walking into the canteen.

'There was an ABCW meeting. So I had to go there,' Avinash replied.

'So, how was the meeting?' asked Prayas.

'Same old shit. But today, I met one of the seniors—Sudeep Sir,' Avinash replied. 'Very decent guy, very supportive. He is also a fan of Bryan Adams like I am and he said he loved me on the guitar when I played during the Fresher's party. For the first time somebody in that group approved of me.'

'Wow, this is the first time you are praising someone from the ABCW. Otherwise, we have only heard people criticizing you for choosing us as your friends,' Ravi said.

'Yeah, but Sudeep Sir is different. The rest of them are morons. They just want me as a part of the group because I am the best guitar player in the college. My being with them helps them flaunt that their guild has talent too!' Avinash retorted.

'Chuck this ABCW business. Let's go to the dhaba!' Prayas suggested.

Later, at the dhaba, they lost themselves in each other's company and cherished their friendship to the strumming of Avinash's guitar and Bryan Adam's 'Summer of '69'.

♦

Institute of Technology & Engineering (ITE), Jhansi
Time: Third Year (2003-04)

'Ravi, guess what?' Prayas said, panting.

'What happened? Why are you running across the institute without catching a breath?' Ravi enquired.

'You know Rishabh Sir, the current secretary of the college? He has asked me to help him in his election campaign for President,' Prayas replied in a single breath.

'If he has asked you, then it means that you will be the Secretary if he wins the election, which he will, since he is already the Secretary. *Teri to life ban gayi!*' Ravi exclaimed.

'Nothing is sure. It's too far-fetched, but I am so glad he asked me to help. I have always looked up to him and his asking me means that I hold a strong position in our batch and among the juniors,' Prayas replied, hiding the fact that Rishabh Sir had already offered him the post of Secretary if he won the election.

'Dude, where were you? I have been looking for you in the

hostel,' Ravi asked Avinash, who was walking towards the canteen.

'I went to meet Sudeep Sir,' said Avinash, joining the other two in the canteen.

'We were talking about the president of the college. And I'm pleased to introduce you to the new secretary of the college!' Ravi broke the news to him.

'Shut up, man. Nothing is decided yet!' replied Prayas, embarrassed.

'What are you guys talking about? Have you had some pegs in broad daylight?' Avinash asked, looking confused.

'Man, Rishabh Sir asked Prayas to help him for his election campaign for the president. That means that he has a very good shot of becoming the secretary of the college!' Ravi replied.

'So what did you say to him?' Avinash asked Prayas.

'Obviously he said yes!' Ravi replied.

'So you will be supporting Rishabh Sir?' Avinash asked Prayas.

'Not just me, but we all will be supporting Rishabh Sir. Are you out of your mind asking these moronic questions?' Ravi replied in an irritated voice.

'No, you two might be. I am not,' Avinash replied.

'What? Then who will you be supporting?' Prayas asked in a startled voice.

'Sudeep Sir. He is also contesting the election. He called me to ask for my help,' Avinash replied.

'But that won't help Prayas achieve his dream of becoming Secretary and further becoming the President. And your Sudeep Sir doesn't even stand a chance of winning against Rishabh Sir!' Ravi replied.

'I can talk to Sudeep Sir for Prayas. I am sure he will agree. I am not supporting Rishabh Sir, no matter what!' Avinash snapped back.

'But what is the problem with Rishabh Sir? He is a nice chap!'

Prayas opened his mouth for the first time in the argument.

'He is a jerk. He is biased against people from the backward category. He slapped and stripped all the people from the backward classes during our ragging, including me, in the first year!' replied Avinash, rage now evident in his voice.

'He slapped me too in the first year, and also made me copy his 23-page-long assignment for him. That was ragging and it is not meant to be taken seriously. I have slapped some juniors during ragging but that doesn't make me a bad person. You are just saying all this because your miniscule brain has been whitewashed by those insecure seniors at the ABCW!' Prayas yelled.

'Miniscule brain? Is that what you guys think about me? You are nothing but autocrats who think that I am not entitled to an opinion. Just because you think that you guys are upper caste, you think I will do anything you like. You just want me to serve my ass on a plate to you as an offering. You guys...' Avinash was shouting, outraged, and before he could continue, Prayas got up from his seat.

'Shut the hell up!' Prayas shouted, slapping him right across the face.

Immediately, Avinash seized Prayas' collar. It was only Ravi who maintained his temper, stopping the two. Avinash left the fight and stomped back to the hostel.

'Are you mad? Why did you have to slap him?' Ravi yelled at Prayas.

'Is he out of his mind? He says we treat him badly because of his caste! You know me. Haven't I always treated him like my younger brother?' Prayas replied, hysterical.

Prayas remembered that as the day his friendship with Avinash ended.

Later in the evening, a few seniors stormed into his room and one of them punched him right in his stomach.

'Arsehole! You think you can slap anyone in the college and walk away? How dare you hit Avinash?'

'Sir, it was just a fight between friends,' Prayas meekly replied. There were two seniors holding him from the back, making it impossible for him to move.

'A fight between friends?' laughed the senior, punching him on the jaw. A thin line of blood trickled from his lips. 'Remember, if you try these heroic stunts of yours on any of the students of our group, I will personally make sure that your face is crooked forever.'

Ravi came running to Prayas' room, got the first aid box and applied Dettol and antiseptic cream on his cut.

'I am not going to leave them. This is it!' said Ravi. 'Come with me.'

'Where? They are seniors! What can we do?' Prayas asked.

By this time, Ravi had taken out his cell phone and was already speaking to someone.

'Hello, Abhishek Bhai? Ravi here. Emergency hai. Can you please come to the college with 4-5 guys? I will meet you at the college gate in half an hour. Bye.' Ravi ended the call.

Then his cell beeped, and there was a message from Avinash which said 'I'm sorry. I didn't ask them to hit Prayas. I was in a foul mood and just had to talk to someone. I didn't know this would happen!'

Ravi deleted the message and took Prayas with him to the main gate of the college. He enquired at the college gate about the seniors who had beaten up Prayas.

'Those jerks have gone to the dhaba. Let's wait for Abhishek Bhai here,' he told Prayas.

'Who is Abhishek Bhai? Why have you called him?' Prayas asked.

'He is a hot shot from University. You will understand when he gets here!' Ravi replied.

Very soon, seven guys arrived on three Royal Enfield motorbikes and stopped right near them. Ravi narrated the incident to them. Ravi asked Prayas to jump onto a bike and they all sped to the dhaba. He saw the seniors who had just hit him sipping pegs of 8PM in the dhaba. Abhishek Bhai went up to the person who had hit him, held him by his collar and kicked him in his groin. The rest of the guys with him started thrashing the others. When they had done enough, Abhishek Bhai picked up the senior, pulled out a revolver from his waistcoat pocket and placed it right under his chin.

'You don't mess with these two again, do you understand? One shot and your entire family will be searching for your dead body and won't be able to find it!' threatened Abhishek Bhai.

'They won't mess with you again and, if they do, keep this with you,' he said, throwing the senior to the ground and handing Ravi the revolver. Ravi took it and kept it in his pocket. Prayas stared at the scene unbelievingly. He had never seen this part of Ravi—fighting and keeping weapons with him, and that too for Prayas's safety.

Prayas had never in his wildest dreams thought that things would get so serious. He had never thought that he would be standing against his best friend for a mere election. Election time closed in and both Prayas and Avinash were on opposite sides, putting in their efforts to support their candidates. Prayas, being the more popular and flamboyant one in college, was the favourite for the post of Secretary.

Prayas's heart broke when the election results were announced and Rishabh had lost the election. The election was close amidst the junior batch, but his own batch was unhappy with Rishabh and voted against him. With Rishabh's defeat, Prayas' dream of being the Secretary and then proceeding to become the President went down the drain. It was like a prick of salt on a wound when Sudeep Sir announced his cabinet and Avinash was declared the Secretary of the college.

Prayas remembered the night the election results were declared. He stayed inside his room for two days without eating, just silently weeping and mourning his political career in ITE, which was over before it could begin. Again it was Ravi who supported him through this difficult time.

'Oye Prayas, let's go to the dhaba,' Ravi said.

'No man, not in the mood.'

'You've been locked in this room for two days without eating. Don't be an idiot. If you don't want to eat, just come and give me company.'

'Okay. Let me wash my face and get ready,' Prayas replied, giving in to his demands.

At the dhaba, all they had were open, heart-to-heart conversations. Ravi joked around and tried to lift his mood. Prayas was feeling better when Ravi brought up the serious topic of elections.

'Bro, what are you planning to do now?' Ravi asked.

'What is left to do now? Avinash is the Secretary already. He has a shot at being the President, not me. My chances are over,' Prayas replied.

'Bro, if Sudeep can topple the current Secretary to become a President, why can't you?' Ravi argued.

'Bhai, that doesn't happen every year and, anyway, I don't want a fight with Avinash. It is finished,' Prayas replied in a defeated tone.

'Rishabh didn't lose the election because you didn't have support. As a matter of fact, you were the one who got it close. It was his own batch that failed him. Your batch and the juniors support you, and you have to increase that support. Regarding Avinash, if he doesn't care and sends seniors to beat the shit out of you, why do you bother?' Ravi asked.

Prayas simply nodded at the argument.

'If you are willing to try, I have a plan. Since you are not the Secretary, you have a lot of leeway in doing things the way you want, side-lining the occasional college rules. I am assuring you that it is possible if you are willing to fight till your last breath,' Ravi added.

'Okay, I will do whatever it takes. I am not going to pass out as a loser who loses once and for all,' Prayas agreed. 'Tell me what I have to do.'

'Nothing as of now. Enjoy the food. We will work on the plan from tomorrow,' Ravi replied.

The next year had passed in a haze. Ravi and Prayas had taken control of the college, or rather, everything that was not official in the college. There were late night dhaba parties with liquor flowing freely and, gradually, the grade IV staffers and clerks were being invited and they tacitly became a part of the group. Soon, Ravi had control of the attendance system and the internal examination papers in the college. Anyone in the junior batch who needed help with attendance or internals was provided help if they confirmed their loyalty to Prayas.

Prayas couldn't believe that without even being in power he and Ravi had become the uncrowned kings of the college. He was shocked to learn how much was possible through a bottle of whisky. He couldn't believe his eyes when Ravi took him for his surprise birthday party. The party had no students, but only the teaching staff who were still bachelors and living alone in their quarters. After that night, the teacher-student relationship was diluted and new friendships were formed. These kinds of teacher-student parties continued on a regular basis on holidays. Suddenly, Avinash's supporters didn't seem to be doing so well in their internals and permission to take leaves for attending meetings and events was being denied. Prayas felt like he was back in the race.

◆

Medical College Hospital, Jhansi
Time: Day after the Election results

Ravi arrived in the hospital by the time doctor had checked Avinash and announced that he was better and out of any kind of danger. Finally, after the doctor permitted them to, Prayas and Ravi entered the room to find Avinash half-sitting on the hospital bed.

'Prayas, Ravi…' his voice wavered on seeing them.

'How are you, bro?' Prayas asked.

'Better. Please forgive me, you two. I was the one who didn't value our friendship,' Avinash spoke.

'Forget it, yaar,' Prayas said.

'No bro, you were the one who carried me here. The doctor told me that I am alive because you brought me here on time. And I was the idiot who was fighting against you and your dream. I am sorry, man,' Avinash continued.

'Shut up, both of you! Let's have a group hug. Are we friends again?' asked Ravi.

'Friends again!' said Prayas, quickly leaping towards Avinash and Ravi.

'Friends,' said Avinash, joining the hug from his bed.

'Now, get well soon so that Prayas can nominate you as his Vice President!' Ravi said to Avinash.

Prayas looked towards him, astonished.

'Are you mad? You should be his Vice President. You were the one who stuck by him!' Avinash replied, equally shocked.

'I have no intention of working for the stupid college. Anyway, I don't have any vices to be a vice president, you know,' Ravi replied.

'Maybe we can create an extra post so that we can all work together!' Prayas suggested, not knowing what else to say.

'Oh please, don't be an idiot. If you guys are so desperate, I will nominate myself for the University Joint Secretary Elections and you two can help me win!' Ravi replied.

'You are kidding, right? University level?' Avinash asked.

Prayas looked towards Ravi with astonishment in his eyes.

'One minute, guys,' Ravi said and walked out to receive a call on his cell phone.

'Hello. Ravi here,' he said.

'Ravi, *Abhishek bol raha hoon* University *se*,' Abhishek Bhai said.

'Yes sir, tell me,' Ravi said.

'What is the status?'

'Go ahead, sir. You can file my nominations for University Joint Secretary. I have the support of the current President and the Leader of the backward classes in the college!' Ravi replied.

'Brilliant! So your gamble finally paid off, Ravi Bhai?' Abhishek jokingly replied.

'*Ab sir, risk toh Spiderman ko bhi lena padta hai. Phir main to university ka Joint Secretary hone ki icha rakhta hoon*,' Ravi laughed back.

'Aha, *dialogue maar rahe ho*! Anyway, I will take care of the paperwork. I will call you if anything is required.'

'Sure sir. Bye,' said Ravi, before hanging up.

He could see Prayas and Avinash sitting on the bed talking to each other as if nothing had happened. His eyes lit up with the glow of a rekindled friendship and the lust to win another election.

Setting

AHMED FAIYAZ

Susheel was busy typing on his laptop. He had to turn in a Business Ethics assignment by 6 pm that day. Even though the college was officially shut for the day, most students had come in. Some wanted to complete and submit their assignments, while some wanted to hang out. The only life that MBA students like him had, was on the campus.

It was a competitive environment at Management Studies Institute, a business school in Gurgaon. All their free time was spent researching companies and contacting the alumni base in Delhi and Gurgaon to try and get job offers. Susheel could not remember the last time he had gone for a movie. Arpit was sitting next to him, waiting for him to finish so that he could copy the assignment, change a few words here and there and submit it. Someone tapped him on his shoulder.

'Excuse me, myself Abhilash Bhisht. This is my good wife Manorama and that's my daughter Anjali,' said a strange man with henna-coloured hair and paan-stained teeth, smiling. He wore a maroon shirt with brown stripes and grey trousers.

'Hello, how are you?' Susheel said, looking up for a moment, while Arpit nodded and smiled. *Maybe he's colour blind*, thought Susheel.

'Jolly good, jolly good. I am the Senior Superintendent of Office Administration at Vikaspur Aluminium. I have come here with family for an office retreat. Can I ask you something?'

I thought they stopped using designations like that. What is he? He might be the boss of tea boys, security staff, drivers and peons. He might even be responsible for buying pens, erasers, ordering business cards and buying toner for the printer. The girl is cute, but appears to be docile. Even if I don't say yes, he's going to ask.

'Sure, go ahead, Mr Bhisht,' Susheel said with a wry smile. Arpit, meanwhile, got busy surfing the Internet, trying to ignore them.

'I am here for an enquiry about admissions. I brought my family to Gurgaon as I was to attend an exhibition hosted by Print On Deskjets. I want my daughter to study here, you see. I heard very good things about this college, top class,' he said emphatically, gesturing with his hands as he spoke.

He, along with his family, was on a fully-paid trip sponsored by a leading maker of toners, cartridges and printers, thanks to all the orders he had placed with them the previous year. It was a case of clandestine bribery in the corporate world.

'Yes, ours is a very good college,' Susheel said.

'*Phourth* rank among all the business schools in India,' Arpit said, with sarcasm, imitating the Dean of the college, at which Mr Bhisht's eyes lit up.

'Bola na, didn't I tell you?' he said with a snort to his wife, who stood there with a morose expression on her face. 'I really want my daughter to get opportunity to study here. Who can I meet and talk to? Procedure kya hai?'

His daughter, Anjali, had a polite smile on her face. It didn't seem like she had anything to do with the decision.

'It's quite a challenging process, uncle. Some 50,000 students apply, after enrolling for CAT, and then only 250 get in, after three rounds of interviews,' Susheel said.

'Less than one per cent, that's only point *phive* per cent,' Arpit added, imitating the good Dean again. Anjali giggled, till her mother turned to her with annoyance. Mr Bhisht looked crestfallen.

He leaned in, putting one arm on the desk, 'Do you know someone, beta? Any setting can be done?'

Arpit looked amused, while Anjali peered over her father's shoulder, looking at Susheel with interest. 'Let me find out, uncle. Give me your email id. I will send you a mail.' Susheel felt that was the easiest way to get rid of him.

'He has a lot of jugaad, uncle. You caught the right guy, he's a member of the Student's Council,' Arpit added for effect.

'What are you saying?' he said with his eyes popping out, leaning closer and putting one hand on Susheel's shoulder. 'Please do something, beta. My Anjali isn't very intelligent like you people, but she works very hard.' Anjali blushed, while the mother moved towards the notice boards with a look of indifference.

'Yes, you see, in a small town like Vikaspur she speaks good English. She even reads English books all the time. What was that… 5 point something by that Champak fellow. She read all this, he also was MBA, na,' he said, rubbing his belly to show off his general knowledge.

'You mean Chetan Bhagat?'

He looked confused, with a worried look on his face. 'Yes, that fellow.'

'Five Point Someone, baba,' Anjali said softly.

'Yes, yes. This and other books on call centres, Americans and Chicken Soup, she read. My Anjali is very modern, she must do MBA.'

'*Phirst* class, uncle,' Arpit said with a smirk.

'You read that book also?' he asked.

'I'm afraid not, uncle. We are very busy with assignments.' *Not over my dead body,* he meant, *his assignment being the next pretty girl he laid eyes on.* 'Our library has some of these wonderful books for intelligent people,' he added with obvious sarcasm.

It seemed like Mr Bhisht remembered only one word from each book title. Needled on by Arpit, he started sweating and gesticulating comically. 'Thank you, yes, see, I said so. Anjali is very smart.'

Anjali, who seemed to get what was going on, looked on, half embarrassed and half amused.

'Can you give me your email id, uncle?' Susheel asked, wanting to get rid of him.

'I don't really use email, you see,' he said worriedly and looked from Arpit to Anjali.

'I can give him my id and keep in touch with him, baba,' Anjali said, smiling sweetly at Susheel.

'Good idea, you take her address and you write to her,' he said spitting out his words, and gesticulating for everything he said, as if he was communicating with the deaf.

'Sure, uncle,' Susheel said, while Anjali pulled out a piece of paper from her diary with her email address written on it and gave it to him.

'Great meeting you, uncle,' Arpit said with a grin, before getting up to give him a firm handshake. He would be blogging about Mr Bhisht in a short while.

'Yes, same here, very nice meeting both of you,' he said with a genuine smile. Anjali smiled coyly and waved before she walked away towards her mother.

'Dude, what a pack of clowns,' Arpit said with a chuckle, slapping Susheel's back.

'He was, but these are small-town people. Anyway, the girl seemed sweet. Quite unlike some of the women we see around here, frivolous and pretentious.'

'Why do you care, man? You can have some fun here. You

can't go and fool around with her, can you?'

'Dude, why is everything about fooling around or sleeping around for you? Your life revolves around it.' Arpit had gone through a string of relationships on and off campus, and couldn't seem to get enough. His latest girlfriend was a girl in their junior batch, with whom he spent hours in the library and the college cafeteria. He even accompanied her to aerobics classes whenever she went.

'Yeah, yeah man, are you done now? I have to go for aerobics in fifteen minutes. Let me copy that file,' Arpit said, turning the laptop towards him, while Susheel looked at the email address on the piece of paper. Anjali had drawn a small heart on top of the 'i' in the id anjali@snailmail.com.

◆

Later that evening, Susheel wrote to her.

> *Hi,*
>
> *It was good meeting you and your family. Contrary to what your Dad thinks, I don't have any "setting" here. You probably have to work very hard and get lucky. I'm happy to offer any advice or help in this direction. I hope you liked visiting this cluster of malls in what used to be a hamlet.*
>
> *Regards,*
> *Susheel*

She responded to his email after three days.

> *Hey,*
>
> *Sorry, we got back only yesterday. It was good meeting you. Your friend was very cool, and very funny. I'm still laughing*

about some of the things he said. My dad is a very simple guy; he doesn't get all this. Thanks for your advice and support. I'm not too keen on doing an MBA but my parents want me to. They feel it'll improve my marriage prospects and help me find a good match. I guess it's a better option than being married off after college. At least I will get to leave Vikaspur and see a bit of the world. I've never been out on my own really. I've been in an all-girls convent and a women's college. It's the get-home-by-6-pm kind of situation here.

What to do? People like me, living in small towns, are stuck in a trap. We tend to keep doing things to lift ourselves out of the small-town mentality but I guess it only sucks us in deeper into that mind-set. Even if they send me to a business school, my parents will only agree to marry me off to someone of our caste, and that too after paying a dowry. Anyway, let's talk about things that are less depressing.

I'm fond of reading actually, and wish to become a schoolteacher. That's why I'm doing a BA, and I hope to start teaching if I don't get into a B-school and if I don't get married off! A big if.

By the way, Champak isn't my favourite author, my Dad doesn't really know. Ha ha. We don't talk much about these things. My favourites are The Painted Veil by Somerset Maugham; Rabbit, Run by John Updike and Jane Eyre by Charlotte Bronte. The last one is my favourite actually.

Maybe your strip of malls on a patch of land would have been fun if I had someone like you showing me around, he he. But no such luck. I just followed my parents from one place to another, though I was allowed to buy a few "modern" dresses, which my mother abhors. She really liked you though, kept raving about how well-mannered you seemed.

Tell me more about yourself. You could be my first friend in a big, bad city. The first boy I can be friends with. What do you like? What are your plans for after your MBA?

Angie

Susheel was pleasantly surprised by her email. It displayed a rare sense of maturity from one he presumed to be a small-town girl with a narrow mind set. He was taken in by her innocence and vulnerability.

He found himself drawn to her and wrote back immediately.

Hey Angie,

It's wonderful hearing from you. It's great to hear a fresh voice from a place which is in the middle of nowhere. Good to know that you're no small-town stereotype. If you want to be a teacher, that's what you should do. I'm a bit busy, but maybe we can chat on the phone or through SMS. My number is 90000000x.

Later,
Susheel

She sent him a text message as soon as she saw his email. Susheel spent every free moment chatting with her. He soon realized that his parents' mind set was no different from her parents'. They wanted their children to grow and break out of their middle-class existence, one he had experienced all his life in East Delhi. Girls had turned up their noses on learning where he lived, and he had worked hard to avoid growing up with an inferiority complex. Anjali, he realized, had lived a similar life with the same challenges and fears of a mediocre existence.

Beyond this, he was taken in by her. The person she was, her coy nature, her simplicity and her values, and her voice. All he wanted to do was to sit and listen to her talk all day. She wasn't the most intelligent girl he had met, but she had no pretensions about herself. He realised that he was falling in love with her. More importantly, he realised that she felt the same.

He made an effort to chat with her as much as he could. They managed to talk on Skype every night after her parents had gone to bed and he had finished his assignments.

◆

6 months later...
In Shimla

Abhilash Bhisht walked out from the lift on to Mall Road, flanked by Manorama and Anjali. Mr Bhisht looked relaxed with his loose polo t-shirt hanging over his belly, and wore a pair of glares. They were on a family holiday after two years. He normally took them to a hill station. Most of the time it was Mussoorie, which was closer, but Shimla had been picked this time around on Anjali's insistence. Her father gave in, considering that she would be getting married in three months and going away to Lucknow.

His wife had dragged Mr Bhisht out to Mall Road finally, after an evening of persistent nagging. Manorama had been left to watch television all day, while her daughter lay in her room and read, and her husband sat drinking beer and munching peanuts in the balcony. He had planned to take them sightseeing on the last two days of their one-week stay. As he stopped to buy popcorn for himself, before his wife dragged him into a store, he spotted Susheel and Arpit. Arpit noticed him as well, and smiled broadly at him.

The boys walked towards the family grinning from ear to ear. 'What luck! We come on our family trip and meet our MBA friends.' He smiled and looked from his wife to his daughter.

'Hello uncle. How are you aunty ji? And you, Anjali ji?' Susheel asked with a smile, almost prostrating in front of them, while the ladies nodded politely as they were expected to.

'We also decided to cool off a bit, uncle. It's extremely hot back in Delhi,' Arpit said. 'We are placed for life too, so nothing to worry about. We've had average salaries of ₹10 lakhs for campus placements this year.'

Mr Bhisht almost dropped his bag of popcorn, his nostrils flared. Manorama's eyes were wide open too. That was more than double what her husband made after twenty-five years in the same company.

'Wonderful, but unfortunately our Anjali didn't get a call from any leading business school. What to do?' he said, twisting his arm forward and gesticulating again. 'But you fellows, ₹10 lakhs a year haan? *Kya baat hai*! Did you hear, Manorama? What did I tell you?' Manorama didn't want to hear anything, she looked pissed off. What she really wanted was to go and spend some of the money her husband made on the side, through backroom deals to replace computers in his company.

Anjali smiled mischievously in the background. She looked demure in a pink and white salwar. Susheel noticed that her cheeks were fuller, and she had grown her hair like he wanted her to.

Finally we meet again, her eyes said to him. He gave her a self-assured smile.

'So you also got a ₹10 lakhs package, haan?' Mr Bhisht asked Arpit.

'I managed a little above average, uncle. Susheel here got double the average. He's placed with an American bank in Mumbai,' Arpit said, patting Susheel's back, as Anjali smiled shyly and Susheel texted furiously on his phone.

'What are you saying? Amrika ka bank, wah! You are special beta, that's fantastic, congrats!' His eyes popped out as he took off his glares and shook hands vigorously with Susheel. Even Manorama displayed her pearly whites this time.

Susheel smiled and took his gaze away from Anjali. Anjali discreetly took out her mobile phone and read the message she had received, 'I love you. You look gorgeous! It's so great to see you again. Soon, it'll be time.' She blushed. Susheel was flirting with her right under her parents' noses. She hadn't even spoken to a boy in front of them, not even her fiancé, a hardware trader who wasn't much to talk to.

A message flashed on his screen, 'I love you too. I can't wait! You don't look too bad yourself. Ha ha … xx …'

They were soon joined by a group of four youngsters. 'Uncle, these are Smita, Sahil and Rohan, our friends from college and Tanya, my sister.'

'Hello, hello ji. So all of you are having fun, haan? That's good, good idea. Before you join the big job with the big salary,' Mr Bhisht said, at which the group faked a laugh and exchanged pleasantries. They glanced at Anjali with interest and gave her a knowing smile; she smiled back.

'So what plans, uncle?' Arpit asked.

'Nothing, yaar. Wife wants to go shopping, so I'm also going.'

'Let the women go shopping, uncle. Why don't you come and sit with us? Our hotel is next door, we can sit at the bar and enjoy a view of the mountains,' Arpit said, taking his arm.

'Acha, but …' he hesitated, looking in his wife's direction.

'Hmmmph, give me money. I'll come with the girls by 7 in the evening,' was her reaction. He moved close to her, handed her a wad of notes and walked away with the boys, while the women moved towards the stores in the opposite direction.

He looked relieved and chirpy, while the guys tried patiently to make conversation. They ordered a round of drinks at the bar and started getting drunk.

'Ma, I just want to stop at the bookstore. Why don't you go ahead with Tanya and Smita? I'll join you at the jewellers after a while.'

'No, I'll come with you,' Manorama insisted.

'I'll go with her aunty, don't worry. I need to pick up a few books too. I'm basically from Shimla. We'll see you at the store later,' Tanya said.

'Yes, please, Ma,' Anjali said as they stood outside New Asia Book Stall.

'Come on, aunty, let these girls be. I know a great place for Kashmiri shawls and pullovers. My uncle knows the owner. We can get a good discount,' Smita said, taking Manorama's hand.

'Okay, don't be late. Your father will lose his mind otherwise,' she said before walking away. She didn't want to deny her girl a little independence; what with her fate being sealed like hers had been over two decades ago.

Anjali merrily nodded and walked away with Tanya.

Susheel, meanwhile, excused himself saying that he had to use the restroom and started to run up to Scandal Point. He took long strides, thinking about his conversation with Arpit an hour ago.

'Are you sure you want to do this?' Arpit asked.

'Yes, I am. I love Anjali, man. There's no one like her.'

'But you've met her only once. She's a small-town girl, born to small-town folk.'

'Dude, I'm sure. I love her despite everything, for the person she is. Sometimes you just know...'

'Your parents?'

'They'll be okay. I can support myself and Anjali. You know

all about the job offer...'

'Cool, so that's fine then.'

'Are all the preparations done?'

'All set, boss.'

The girls strode up the stairs by the church, where a worried-looking Susheel was waiting for them. 'Thank God you guys made it,' he said as he embraced Anjali and kissed her on her forehead, while Tanya called the driver on her phone. They stood there for a while, locked in an embrace, as young honeymooners looked on, and kids pointed at them.

'Susheel, get on with it,' Tanya said. 'All the best,' she added, as Susheel and Anjali rushed out holding hands.

◆

2 hours later...

'Oh hello aunty, how was your shopping? Hope you enjoyed yourself,' Tanya said, meeting her outside Shyam Lal's.

'Yes, thank you beta. But where is Anjali? She called me some time back saying she was going to your house.' Manorama looked tense, besides from being tired from all the shopping.

'Yes aunty, she had a splitting headache, you see. That's why I took her home. She didn't want to trouble you and disturb your shopping plans. She's okay now, she's asleep. I'll bring her back tomorrow morning. She spoke to you right?'

'Yes, but my poor child, I want to see her,' she screeched. *Shit*, thought Tanya.

'Relax aunty, she's well taken care of, and you must be tired. Tanya's house is in Naldhera, it's going to be difficult to go there now. It's past seven, let's go and see how uncle is,' Smita said. She seemed to have taken to Smita, who had put up with her all evening.

'Okay, but I don't know what he's going to say.'

They walked down to the hotel hoping that everything was okay. Manorama didn't notice Susheel's absence at the bar and walked up to her husband who was in an inebriated state. He was regaling the boys with his hoarse rendition of Jagjit Singh's ghazals.

'Wife, come and sit here. Sing with me,' he shouted.

'What is this? You're drunk!'

'What I do otherwise? You want me to read newspaper here haan? Where is Anjali?'

'She had a headache. I've taken her to my house, uncle. We'll bring her back tomorrow morning.'

'I see, okay. Do you ladies want beer?' Manorama, though relieved, gazed at him with irritation.

'Come uncle, we'll drop you back. My car is downstairs,' Arpit said, as he gestured to Mr Bhisht to rise from the stool he was perched on.

'Where is Susheel?' he asked looking around with his bloodshot eyes, his breath reeking of beer.

'Stomach upset, uncle, bad stomach,' Arpit said.

Mr Bhisht looked amused. 'Okay good night,' he said with a slur to the boys, before he hugged them and followed his wife and Arpit out.

◆

'Mr Bhisht, good morning. This is Tanya and Arpit's father, Ajit Malhotra. How are you?'

'Yes, Arpit…I remember.' His head was splitting with a bad hangover. He sat up in his boxers. His wife seemed to be in the shower. 'Your son is very nice fellow. How are you?'

'I'm fine thanks. Your daughter, Anjali, is here and there seems to be a matter that we have to discuss. I have sent my driver to your hotel. He should be there soon. Please come down here.'

'Is Anjali okay?' He remembered that his daughter had not come back last night. It was something that had never happened in the past.

'Yes, she is. See you soon, Mr Bhisht.'

After an hour, they got out of the car, admiring the Malhotras' sprawling estate. They walked into the heritage villa and across the lawn to be greeted by Tanya, who took them to the visitors seating area.

Mr Malhotra, a tall, well-built gentleman exuding sophistication and fine upbringing, walked in with Anjali and Susheel. She wore a red salwar dress and he wore an ethnic suit. She had a tika on her forehead and a wedding ring on her finger. The rest of the group followed them into the room, as Mr Bhisht stood there looking enraged, while Anjali clung on to Susheel's arm.

'What, this fellow...'

'Mr Bhisht, Susheel and Anjali love each other. They got married at a temple in town last night, with the blessings of our family. They spent the night here, and early this morning we got the marriage registered. The certificate should be here tomorrow. Now, Susheel is a good boy and they did what they had to. I'll leave the four of you to talk this out.'

Mr Bhisht looked away. He couldn't match Mr Malhotra in his words and persona. He was overwhelmed by the man, awed by his towering presence. Manorama's expression was back to being morose.

Mr Malhotra and the group walked out of the room and shut the door.

'What is your full name?' Mr Bhisht asked with a flash of anger in his eyes.

'Susheel Punjabi, uncle. We are from East Delhi. My father runs an STD booth and an internet parlour. I have a younger sister.'

'Punjabi! How could this be? What will happen…'

'You keep quiet ji! What will happen? So what if he's Punjabi and we are not? The boy is okay, you were the one who was falling over him and praising him. He is educated and has a job offering him more money than you make. We don't have to give him the money we saved all our lives to marry our girl.'

'But she is engaged! What about that Upadhayay fellow? We gave our word…'

'She's married now,' Manorama shouted. 'We call and say that she marry better fellow, more educated, decent.'

Susheel smiled. For the first time since he had known her, she was standing up against her husband.

'I love him, Baba,' Anjali said, with her hand in Susheel's looking meekly at him.

'Okay, what I say now?' Mr Bhisht said, at which Manorama beamed and embraced the couple.

◆

2 days later
In Delhi

'Why did you have to even come back? You should have stayed with your godfather Malhotra,' his father thundered as he paced up and down the room.

Susheel had brought Anjali home a short while earlier and announced his surprise marriage to his hapless parents. His mother, a short but stout woman with soft features, stood there sizing up Anjali, looking at what she wore and her mannerisms. Anjali looked worried and tears started rolling down her cheeks when the shouting began.

'You are my parents, that's why I came back. We're married now, why do you want to create a scene?'

'Scene? Look at your son, this is his audacity haan? He thinks this is a joke. Is this why I borrowed money and sent him to do an MBA? So that he can do what he pleases and marry whom he wants?'

'I'm 25. Look, relax, papaji. You have a heart problem. She's a very nice, educated girl, look at her. She's beautiful too. She's not from my college; she's a nice girl from Vikaspur...'

'I'm not concerned. Who do you think you are?'

'Papaji' she's my wife now, that isn't going to change. I'll return all the money you spent on my MBA doesn't mean you can dictate my life. I can live life on my own terms and provide for her.'

'Return my money, oye? Haan ji, you're a big shot now! You got a job at an American bank. This is why you're throwing your weight around. Get out oye, leave my house.'

'Yes, I don't care, I'm going...' Susheel took Anjali's hand in his and started to pick up her suitcase.

'Wait,' the mother said. She pulled the father into the bedroom.

'Is this what you raised the boy for? He's our only son, he's worked hard. Who'll look after us when we grow old? Who will marry your daughter? Finally we have a grown-up son, so we don't have to break our backs. Just when he is settling down and doing well, you ask him to get out!' She stood with her arms on her hips, as he cooled down.

'Look at the way he spoke to me!'

'He's come home with his bride, and you're insulting him. He's a young man, he isn't going to take it. Go out there and be reasonable now.'

'But he should have asked us, shouldn't he? This is all the josh of the job he's got.'

'What are you going to do? Send him away and not talk to him. You want to make your son your enemy and sit in an STD booth all your life? Isn't his happiness important?'

'Hmmm…Yes, his happiness is important. What can we do now? I'm old, I don't have strength in me anymore,' he said, holding his chest.

Mr Punjabi came out of the room and looked from his son to his daughter-in-law. 'Hmmph, come here oye, ithe aao, both of you,' he said with open arms.

'Why are you standing like an idiot? Take her bags to your room,' his mother said to Susheel, as she put her hand on her daughter-in-law's head.

Susheel's phone rang a few minutes later. 'Hi, yes this is Susheel Punjabi.'

'Susheel, this Carol Smith from the bank. I head the HR Department for South Asia and the Middle East. How are you?'

'Yes, it's good to hear from you. I'm fine ma'am.'

'Is this a good time?'

'Yes, it is.'

'I'm afraid there's some bad news. We regretfully have to withdraw the offer made to you. Faced by the recession in the U.S., and given our weak position due to foreclosures, we've been bought out by another bank. We are shutting down our South Asian operations immediately.'

'What? How…'

'I'm sorry, Mr Punjabi. I wish you all the very best. You're a very capable young man. This is an unfortunate situation for all of us. I wanted to call you myself…' He sat down, turning on the television and switching to a business news channel.

'Bloodbath on Wall Street', the headline screamed, while Carol Smith's voice faded in the background.

'The assets of Boston Global Bank were today acquired by Bank of Phoenix, resulting in fears of job losses of over 10,000...' the anchor said, while the bank's logo and images of its head office in Boston flashed on the screen.

Susheel was the only one with eyes and ears glued to the television, while the others were consumed in their own excitement.

'Go bring 10 boxes of sweets,' his father said to the boy who worked in the shop, pulling out his wallet to empty it of its contents.

'This has all been so sudden. Let me take you tomorrow and buy you jewellery,' his mother said to his beautiful bride, who smiled shyly as she gazed dreamily at Susheel. His mother started making phone calls to relatives.

'This is wonderful bhaiya, we should throw a huge party,' his teenage sister said, walking into the room as he tried to comprehend what had just happened.

Dreams of an apartment in South Bombay, a honeymoon in Paris, a diamond pendant for his wife, a brand new Honda City, quickly evaporated as the news of his withdrawn job offer sank in and he stared blankly at the paint peeling off the walls of the sparse living room.

Lights Out

Just a Moment

NIKHIL RAJAGOPALAN

I finally put the pen down and glanced around. It was my final exam for my baccalaureate degree and I felt that I had finished a little too early—about half an hour earlier than the stipulated three hours. There was an eerie silence throughout the classroom but there were sounds of laughter and high-fives being exchanged outside. This stark contrast made me more nervous. I saw students slinging on their backpacks while others picked up their suitcases, chatting all the while. Judging by the lively atmosphere, they weren't the least bit concerned about acing the final exam; they seemed happy to just be done with it. And guessing by the suitcases and the traveller's backpacks that they brought to the exam hall, they had a train or plane to catch that night. I smiled to myself. Why not? I had done the exam to the best of my abilities and I wasn't the type to look back on this moment with regret; second guessing that had I used the precious time left, perhaps, just perhaps, my grade point average wouldn't have dipped by point five and caused my master's application to crash out of Harvard in a ball of flame.

I took one last look at my answer sheets and stood up resolutely handing them over to the examiner I then thanked him, collected my belongings and walked out of the hall.

It was done.

Four years of sweat had finally paid off. I took a moment to recollect the late nights I had spent at the computer centre working on my C++ code as part of mandatory computer training, the molecular biology lab sessions that stretched way beyond 6 pm and never yielded any results and the seemingly never ending cancer biology classes. And as the moment quickly passed, I was engulfed by the happy banter and loud laughter of my peers. The invigilator stepped outside and told us to clear off, but not without smiling. He was happy to see us graduate and to be rid of us as well. Happiness is indeed such a complex and multi-faceted emotion.

I went back to the hostel since I knew the food court would be full to bursting with ecstatic final year students. I met a few friends on the way who couldn't stay to chat as they had to take the six o'clock train to Chennai and then make it to the airport to catch a flight early the next day. Dusk was approaching, the crows were heading back to their nests and the sun would soon be sinking into the horizon.

Ah, good old 213! I let myself in, locked the door behind me and tossed the keys on the table. I took the iPod out of my pocket and plugged it in to my speakers and selected a mellow track. I eased back on the pillow and fished out the crumpled hall ticket from my back pocket and laughed at the photo of myself that the University had chosen to print on it. I was never photogenic to begin with, but this one—with my slightly skewed glasses and frizzled hair—took the cake. I smoothed out the creases, put the ticket down beside me and took out my copy of *Norwegian Wood* by Murakami and picked up where I had left off. Coldplay's 'Parachutes' faded and was replaced by King of Leon's 'Charmer'. I read for a good hour with my eclectic collection playing gently (and not so gently during Machine Head's 'Halo') in the background.

At half past seven, I made my way downstairs to the mess and sat down for dinner. The mess was quite empty courtesy the mass exodus of students, but I didn't see the second or third year students

either. I ate my dinner in silence and looked for any familiar faces
at the other tables. I found none. After dinner, back in my room,
I boiled water and made some coffee for myself in my favourite
brown mug (the one my distantly related uncle gave me before
he passed away) and sipped the dark brew while observing the
juniors playing badminton in the quadrangle below. Some of the
other rooms on my floor were locked; their (erstwhile) residents
whom I'd known for three long years now gone in a matter of
moments. I sighed and went back to my room, slamming the door
behind me. I had taken a two-day extension, so I could vacate the
hostel by Friday. I could have been done by tomorrow like the rest
of the students, but I wanted to be in my sanctuary for another
two days if I could help it. The cardboard boxes in the corner
demanded my undivided attention. I had grown attached to this
room over the years and this was my personal space: my secret
hideout, my Fortress of Solitude, my Bat-Cave. I bought my PC in
my second year and had even skipped classes one day just so that
we could set up our (illegal) local area network which, in essence,
was tossing two metres of LAN cables out our windows to the
room with the router on the ground floor. We would play World
of Warcraft and Counterstrike over the network and it wouldn't
be at all surprising to hear, 'Fire in the hole!' or rapid bursts of
simulated gunfire at half past two in the morning. I looked out my
window, still nursing my coffee. There was a beautiful view of the
E-Block hostel accompanied by a perfect view of the sunrise. But
that was two years ago. In keeping with the pace of construction
that matched the fervour of the Blitzkrieg, a new student hostel
sprung up between our hostels and took away my view. Now instead
of beautiful sunrises, I'm greeted by the sight of sleepy hostellers,
their mouths frothing with toothpaste. Not the most enchanting
thing to see, I assure you. I started with the posters first. I took

down my posters of Avril Lavigne, Nelly Furtado and Bon Jovi with the greatest care. I packed the textbooks and photocopies (no degree is complete without photocopied hand-outs) and placed them into the boxes and placed others in a pile that I decided to donate to the library. Next I disassembled the PC and put the monitor and the CPU in their respective boxes. The progress was slow and every action was done with deliberation, as I still couldn't believe my time had come to say farewell to room 213. I sat back on the bed, surprised at the attachment I'd developed to this place. It was just a room after all. No one had heard of someone getting sentimental over real estate.

A sharp rap at the door brought me to my senses and I went to answer it. It was Krish, my close friend who lived in room 206.

'Fancy giving me a hand packing? I've got to head out tomorrow evening and I haven't exactly started.'

I hoisted myself off the bed and put my iPod on pause. 'Sure. I was sort of doing the same myself.'

Locking up the room, we went over to Krish's place. The room was a right mess: sports magazines were stacked in piles in the cupboard, posters of Zeppelin and Metallica adorned the wall and the table was littered with empty packets of crisps and miscellaneous stationery. In the corner lay strewn clothes and sachets of detergent. I swore loudly. Krish took this as a good sign.

'Glad to have you on-board, Captain,' he said wistfully.

'Has the Department of Health given you clearance for this place?' I questioned casually.

'Ever the funny one, aren't you, Nick? C'mon, give me a hand with the magazines and the posters.'

We spent about an hour and half cleaning up. Of course we digressed a lot over the course of it, like we always did. We ended up reading a few articles from the magazines we were supposed to put away, had an argument over the existence of God and played air guitar to 'Stairway To Heaven'. It was way past ten and the warden had done his rounds, knocking at each occupant's door and putting down a little check beside their name on his register. The hostel was quiet save for the silent hum of the air-conditioners and the occasional yelling that was to be expected when someone's rear end was handed to them in an adrenaline pumping match of Counterstrike. Krish sat down on his bed, while I took his chair.

'I'm going to miss this place,' he said and I could sense the slight break in his voice. I said nothing, while Krish bent over and retrieved something from under the bed.

'We're going to celebrate,' he said, bringing out a box of green tea.

'And I thought it was going to be alcohol,' I said with a laugh.

'Yep. The good stuff for a good occasion, you reckon?' We cleaned up two ceramic mugs and made two piping hot cups of green tea.

'Oh, goodness. We forgot to toast!' I said.

'Yes. Let's toast to four years here, our last exam, our friendship and, most important of all, the mess you're helping me clean up right now,' Krish suggested. We sipped again, the tea working its warm magic as it slid down my throat.

'So what becomes of us now?' he asked. 'I don't know,' I said. I was so caught up in the journey that I hadn't thought about what would happen once the train stopped at its destination.

'This was so much easier in school, you know? Once you finished second grade, you moved onto third grade. You knew where you were headed. Heck, we all did. God, I love linearity,' Krish sighed.

'But now comes this feeling of uncertainty; the unavoidable pressure to decide what you're going to do with the rest of your life. Do I get a job? Do I study for a master's degree? Should I marry in a few years and have two kids and name them Divya and Avinash?' he said, in a weary tone.

'I hear you. It feels like I'm at a crossroads. I see many signs that point me in different directions. But which road do I take? And more importantly, even if I walk down the path I've chosen, how can I tell if I've chosen correctly?' I said, sipping the hot tea gently.

'Oh man, this is heavy stuff,' said Krish, pulling out a pack of cigarettes. We opened up the windows and let the fresh air in. We got a beautiful view of the road that connected the hostels, bathed in streetlight. Krish lit up and offered me one even though he knew I didn't smoke. That was just the kind of guy he was.

'I've been studying for the GRE for months now. I've sneaked the Barron's into every class, studied into the wee hours of the morning and I'm even listening to vocabulary lists on my iPod,' he said. He was going to take his exam next week in Bangalore and had made known his fear that no university would accept him for the pathetic scores he was expecting to get. 'I mean Anish got a 1420 and didn't make the cut last year!' I knew about our unlucky senior, but things sometimes went your way, though I couldn't tell Krish about that. Not now, anyway.

He exhaled and a cloud of smoke hung lazily over our heads, much like our worries and our inhibitions.

'And you?' he asked me, still gazing out the window.

That was a good question. I had taken the GRE already and scored a lousy 1290. I had applied to seven universities in the States with tentative mark sheets and had no idea if any of them would accept me. They saw me as just another silhouette. They had to gauge everything that was quintessentially me from a series of exams, aptitude tests and statements of intent. They didn't even ask for a photograph, for crying out loud.

'I don't know. I've gone through the motions. I'm playing the waiting game now,' I said sombrely.

'You want to get back to packing, Nick?'

'No.'

'Me neither.'

'So what *do* you want to do?' I asked him.

He didn't say anything for the longest time. At last he stubbed out his cigarette and looked at me.

'I wish I could stay in this moment a while longer. Just a while longer,' said Krish.

We drank the last of our tea in silence with the hum of air-conditioners all around us.

Learning and Unlearning

ROHINI KEJRIWAL

'Be quiet or Akka will come and catch us,' said Alisha, peeping out of the Box Room door and checking to see if our houseparent's light came on. Her light being on meant that our noise levels had risen beyond the permissible point and that she had been woken up from her beauty sleep and would now come to the source of the noise to scold the ruckus-makers. Tonight was not one of the nights when we could get into trouble only for the noise. A Maggi party was in session.

Making Maggi in a boarding school is an illegal but sacred act. You must know exactly what you are doing—who is going to cook it, who is heating the water, who is cleaning after the act of consumption takes place, and who keeps the deodorant at hand, a precautionary measure to get rid of the smell in case the houseparent comes to do her rounds. There are big bowls in which the evening snack is served. Someone clears out the contents of one such bowl, washes it, and hands it to the cook. The cook crushes an 'n' number of cakes of noodles ('n' being a variable for the number of people present), and pours the proportionate amount of hot water which is brought from the solar water tap. The bowl is covered with another plate and left to 'semi-cook'.

After ten minutes or so, the water is drained out, (burning the hands of the one draining it) the masala is sprinkled over the steaming noodles, and after the cook mixes it with her hands, everyone digs in! The consumption is almost always with the hands since otherwise spoons have to be flicked from the Dining Hall (DH). The person who washes the bowl usually gets to lick it clean of the masala before washing up. Quite a treat, I assure you! In the end, the deodorant is sprayed, the fan is left on and everyone returns to their rooms as though they were in no way associated with any illegal incidents that day. Sadly, too many people got caught keeping illegal foods and no one practises such nights anymore.

This Maggi Party was unlike others in the past. It was the last one as school students. A few hours ago had been our Farewell Night. The Farewell Night, as always, was during the middle of the Board exams for some, and almost towards the end for some of the Science students. It was on a Saturday so that no one was worried about an examination the next day. The girls wore beautiful saris in varying hues of blue, green and orange. The boys were either wearing tucked-in shirts or kurtas. In a few days, the 12thies would have to vacate the classroom we had gotten so fond of and head out into different parts of the world, pursuing our different dreams. Some knew which direction they were heading in. Others could only hope that they would stumble upon their paths soon.

Goodbyes were said by the teachers and house parents first. Then, the stage was open to students to give their farewell speeches. We share our farewell with the 10thies because some of them leave for other schools for their plus-2, while others will not be called back. For the 12thies, it is a definite parting... A parting that I did not make too willingly. I had my speech in my hand. Usually, I would write down my thoughts and feelings for an occasion such as this one. This time, I found what I had to say in the words of another. I read out something from Jon Krakauer's *Into the Wild,* which aptly described my state of mind at the time:

Still, the last sad memory hovers round, and sometimes drifts across like floating mist, cutting off sunshine and chilling the remembrance of happier times. There have been joys too great to be described in words, and there have been griefs upon which I have not dared to dwell; and with these in mind I say: Climb if you will but remember that courage and strength are naught without prudence, and that momentary negligence may destroy the happiness of a lifetime. Do nothing in haste; look well to each step; and from the beginning, think what may be the end.

Soon, the speeches ended, some people broke down and the tedious process of consoling 'senti' batchmates began. It dawned on everyone that this was *it*. We'd attended other Farewell Nights in the past few years where we had been listening to the speeches. But tonight, we were the ones saying our goodbyes to our fellow batchmates, juniors, teachers, and even to the wonderful Principal who called me a 'hyper little squirrel' and would accuse me of not bathing when my hair was messy.

I rushed out of the hall as the nostalgia started to hurt. I found myself walking back to the hostel hastily, almost tripping on the 2-inch heels that I had been practising walking on for the last two weeks. My tears were not going to be on public display tonight. I went to the backyard to wash my face and almost jumped when I saw her sitting alone in a corner, crying. She was the only girl I had been afraid of in my class. She was always in baggy jeans and loose shirts that ought to be worn by boys, had the most intimidating glare, and was weirdly allergic to fruits. She was a senile creature according to most, and was possibly the only person in school to not even have a friend whom she could call her own.

She looked extremely weak suddenly. She sat crouched against the wall in a black sari, allowing tears to flow out of those perpetually angry eyes. I was witnessing her in a moment of weakness. I walked up to her, not thinking about what I was doing, and opened my arms to her; a part of me was scared that she would take them and twist them or something. She leaned in for the hug, much to my surprise. 'Don't mention this to anybody or it won't be good for you,' she whispered, letting go almost as soon as she let our bodies meet.

'I won't. Do you want to talk?' I asked, trying to help her break the façade she had created for herself and let me in. 'Have you ever climbed the terrace at night?' she asked, taking me by surprise, and on seeing me shake my head, she grabbed my hand forcefully and led me to the washing area from where we'd climb up to the terrace on Saturdays and eat tamarinds. Before I knew it, two strangers in saris were lying on a terrace that revealed the wonders of the night sky. To kill the awkwardness that was rising in my mind, I kept a look out for a shooting star.

She was the one who broke the silence. She told me that she was afraid of leaving this place, of losing the sense of familiarity she felt on seeing the faces of her 'dorky classmates', of being sucked into the apparently big, bad world where crimes were rampant. She confessed that she wanted to break out of her shell and let people know her as the person she was, but was too scared to actually let that happen. Her uncle beat her up and molested her almost every day as a child, and though her parents knew about it, they never acted upon it. The uncle brought home the bread, and her parents were indebted to him for his 'kindness'. She yearned for a mother's love and a father's words of wisdom. She wanted to feel. But she couldn't. She wanted to speak up. But she couldn't.

I remember crying with her that night. I remember feeling a chill run down my spine despite the heat of the March night. I remember her face going pale as she told me. I remember how hard it was for her to speak. I remember the silences in the middle of sentences, followed by a stream of tears and barely audible sobs. I remember the hug we shared after she had told me what she had wanted to. She felt unburdened and her lips gave away her sense of relief.

I half wished that this was some surreal dream I had been having. But there was no waking up needed. The only thing I woke up to was her reality. A reality, I realized, that she had to deal with completely alone in her other life. They say that a child in a boarding school leads two lives—one as a student/sibling/child in the boarding school with his batchmates, roommates, and houseparents; the other back home as a member of his/her blood family. In her eyes, she had no family in either life, but this was her 'home'. More than the people, the place had given her solace and something to relate to, to keep her grounded. While I was afraid of losing touch with the people I had gotten to know in my four years there, she was afraid of sinking into a deep, dark hole in unfamiliar territory. The people did not matter to her and faces had been a blur for too long a time. For her, the hills, the lone walks to the gate, the trees under which she sat and read Tolstoy, and the well in the Veg Garden would be left behind. A different farewell would be said, a different set of memories would be taken.

She finished what she had to say and got up. 'Goodbye... And thank you,' she said, walking away, her back to me. I knew that she would not look me in the eye after this. She would not say goodbye before she left. She had let someone in too close and, despite the momentary relief she got from doing so, this revelation of her inner self would bother her. I looked up at the star-strewn sky. I would feign indifference to her in our last few days here. She would prefer it to be that way. But what I would do secretly would be to leave a letter in her suitcase, telling her that she had 'someone' if she ever needed a hug or a shoulder, and if she wanted to get in touch with that 'someone', how and where she could do so. It is no surprise that the 'someone' has still not heard from her.

There are some things that one knows for a fact; there are others that are assumed to be facts but must be unlearnt in order to truly learn them.

The Worm That Turned

MALATHI JAIKUMAR

'Walk along with the coolie. Don't lose sight of him. Look for Coach A2. Watch out…Your shoulder bag is about to fall!'

Vishnu walked faster. Instructions, instructions all the time. That was his mother. The more distance between him and his family, the better. They were the ones who had delayed him, leaving barely enough time to catch the train. Darn. The shoulder bag had to fall, just to prove his mother right!

He almost dashed against another passenger rushing the other way and heard a voice again—it was his father this time, 'Can't you look where you are going, Vishnu?'

The Tamil Nadu Express was a metal anaconda, stretching interminably. The platform was seething with humanity of all shapes, sizes and colours with a variety of baggage to match. Like pet dogs that tend to resemble their owners, the luggage reflected their carriers. Unwieldy bundles and jute bags went into unreserved compartments, worn out suitcases held together by thick ropes or much used holdalls went into the ordinary sleeper class while suitcases, trolley bags and backpacks went into the AC Sleeper or AC First Class.

The coolie stopped short and Vishnu almost fell backwards trying to avoid crashing into him. The family was not far behind. 'I am sure you have two left feet'—that was Little Miss Know-it-All, his sister.

He ignored her and concentrated on loading his luggage. It was a coupe cabin right at the head of the compartment. An old man of about 75 was already seated on the lower berth. He was tall and thin, dressed in well worn, comfortable looking, grey corduroy pants and a checked shirt. He had a good head of white hair and sharp, beady eyes under bushy eyebrows.

Vishnu's parents struck up a conversation immediately.

'Are you going to Delhi?' *Where else would the Tamil Nadu Express go? To Timbuktu?*

'Yes.'

'Oh good. This is our son. He has never stirred out of Chennai and is going to Delhi for the first time to join St. Stephen's College.' There was a touch of pride in his father's voice.

'Appa...' protested Vishnu, wishing he was invisible.

'You keep quiet. He is very modest you know. He scored the highest marks in his college. But he is very shy and very gullible. I am glad you are here. Please look after him...'

Vishnu squirmed. He was busy polishing his thick, black-framed glasses that were almost knocked off as his sister hustled closer, grasping his arms, to give him last minute tips.

'Be careful in Delhi. Punjabis are much shrewder than us South Indians.'

He wished his family had been born dumb.

'Especially the girls—watch out for them. Do not be taken in by them, Anna. They are not like your Ambujam, your scrawny, pig-tailed, Maths friend.'

'I think you should go now. It will take you more than an hour to get back home.' He tried to push them out before all the passengers heard about his love life or rather the lack of it.

'Don't eat Punjabi food. It is all oily and full of fat. You have such a weak stomach. Starts the runs at the drop of a hat.'

Vishnu groaned inwardly. After personal history, they were now broadcasting his medical history. It was a toss-up as to which was more embarrassing.

'Look after your money. They are all thieves. They can fool you easily.'

By now he had managed to get them near the door. As they got out, one by one, the train began to move very slowly. They all scurried along shouting, 'Send us emails every day.'

He nodded, waved to his family and turned away only to catch the parting shot from his mother, loud and clear, for the whole station to hear. 'Wash your chuddies personally. You never know what infections others have.'

He tried to pretend they were not his family.

As soon as he entered the compartment, the old man's eyes followed his every move. Vishnu avoided eye contact, quickly made his bed on the upper berth and clambered up. With a huge sigh of relief he settled down. He had had enough of his family to last him for months. All he wanted was some peace and quiet. He fished out one of the books from the *Urban Shots* series from his backpack and soon lost himself in the interesting medley of short stories.

Next morning, he woke up dreading going down and having to chat with the old man. There would be more advice and boring old tales of long ago and the 'good old times'. Strange how good times were always in the past, never in the present. However, short of jumping off the train, there was no escaping the old man. He had a whole day of travel left and he would have to come down sometime.

'So this will be your first taste of campus life?'

'Yes.'

'You have to be brave and calm.'

'Hmm.'

'But not cocky... Not too confident. That always gets their goat.'
'Hmm.'
'I knew somebody just like you. It is a very interesting story.'
Vishnu remained silent. But that was no deterrent.
'It was in Calcutta. Jadavpur University. They were a wild lot and this was The Boy's first day. Those days the ragging went on for months together, not just for the first few days.'
Oh God. Not another ragging story, thought Vishnu. That was all he had heard about this past month. Everyone in the world had a favourite ragging story.
There was no stopping the old man. 'The Boy was the most 'popular' target because he suffered each and every torture silently. He did everything that was asked of him, not only uncomplainingly but willingly. They were constantly trying to rile him and he refused to rise to the bait. He was made to roll in the mud, propose to five girls from the college opposite to theirs, lick his senior's boots, enact some pretty stupid scenes like making love to a pillow...'
Would he have to listen to hackneyed ragging stories for half the journey? Maybe he could pretend to be sick.
'What they did not know was that The Boy's life so far had been one long session of ragging almost on an everyday basis. He was picked on by his family, friends and teachers. His appearance, his manner and his attitude just cried out to be mocked at and he had accepted it as the norm. In fact, the day he was not ragged was not worth living.'
Vishnu wondered if the old geezer would ever come to the point.
'When, even after a month and a half, The Boy never rebelled or protested, and complied with all their demands, they decided on one final assault. He was asked to sneak into the women's college opposite, enter a girl's room, kiss her and get her to sign a paper

affirming that she had been kissed. He then had to strip down to his underpants, leave his clothes behind and return to his room, walking out in full view of everyone, across the campus. If he was caught he would be in serious trouble with the authorities of both colleges. If, however, he could pull it off, he would be accepted not only as one of their own, but would be treated with all the respect due to a leader. He was given a week to plan and execute his mission.'

Vishnu turned around to face the old man. Now the story was getting more interesting. Much to his irritation, the man got up slowly, put up his little finger and went out. Fifteen minutes later he returned, leaned back and closed his eyes. It was almost as if he had forgotten that he was in the middle of a story.

Vishnu waited and fidgeted and ultimately burst forth, 'And then what happened, sir?'

'What?' The old man woke up with a start, 'Oh. I have a prostrate problem. It always takes a long time.' Vishnu felt like shaking the man. Was he being dense on purpose? Or was he teasing him?

'I meant what did the Boy do?'

'Aaah…' He sat up straight, took off his glasses, polished them, put them on again and cleared his throat. 'He knew that this was the final test. So he spent most of the week planning. You see, he had a passion for history and, with his head for detail, there was very little he did not know about wars and strategies. Although he did not look it, he had the makings of one of the greatest generals ever. Besides, fortune favours the brave.

'On the very first day of his arrival he had seen the girl standing outside the college. She was not stunningly beautiful, but there was something about her that made her stand out in a crowd. Perhaps it was the way she held her head, the tips of her light brown hair falling just short of her perfectly shaped breasts, her understated style of dressing, her bee-stung lips, or maybe even her dramatic eyes that were dark pools of melancholy. She seemed to move in a world of her own, a world bereft of all joy. He longed to go across and comfort her or speak a few words of kindness, to let her know that she was not alone in her misery. He had never felt this way before, but he did not have the gumption to break the ice. Not yet.

'She was one of the five girls he had proposed to as one of his "Tasks of Hercules" as he called the ragging episodes. While the other girls smiled, giggled or made fun of him when he proposed, she looked deep into his eyes as if she was searching for something. After a whole two minutes, when the world around him ceased to exist, she gently shook her head and said slowly and seriously, as if she had considered his proposal very thoroughly, "Not now. Not yet. Maybe later." This was met by hoots of laughter and more teasing but The Boy knew she had meant every word—and was further intrigued.

'Ever since that day, he had kept a watchful eye on her and her movements. He noted the time she went on her walks alone, the number of the car that came to pick her up each Saturday morning and drop her back the same evening. On Sundays, when all the other girls were going in and out, she stayed in her room.

'Then he began waiting for her at a particular spot on her regular walking route. He never dared to do more than watch her walk by, and she never showed by a glance or a flicker of her melancholic eyes that she knew he was there. Then one day, after a week, he silently joined her on the walk, quaking inside, quite sure that she would send him packing. Surprisingly, she just looked at him and went on walking without missing a step, as if he was not visible. Silent walks soon became a routine. No words were spoken, just strides that matched each other's.

'Now, with the final challenge weighing him down, he could not keep quiet. On the next walk, he unburdened himself. Her deadpan face showed no glimmer of interest, but gradually he could see her take sidelong glances at him with a calculating look on her face.

'The next day she broke her silence. "Come to my room next Sunday at 1 pm. I will inform the chowkidar that my cousin will be visiting. You do not have to kiss me. I will sign a paper confirming that you did and, what's more, I will get the other four girls to sign it too. They quite like you, you know? It is a myth that girls like macho men. They also like geeks with spunk or, should I say, punks with spunk." A hint of a smile touched her lips. His heart flipped over. If he could make her smile, he had touched a chord in her.

'But he found the plan far too easy and suspicious. He wondered if this was a trap set up by some of the boys who knew this girl. He was annoyed with himself for doubting her, but life had made him wary of everything and everyone. He had to do something very convincing and dramatic to put an end to the whole issue, and he had to do it himself.

'The little General decided that surprise was an essential factor, as essential as a detailed knowledge of the ground. On the appointed day, he waited till 11 pm to creep out of bed, clad all in black. There were eight rooms in his wing, two students per room. His roommate was blissfully oblivious to everything; thanks to the two tablets of Alprax the Boy had slipped into his glass of Horlicks. He knew it would be effective as he had seen his mother getting knocked out.

'The Boy padded silently to each room and slid the bolts on the outside. No one would be able to get out in a hurry. He then made his way to the fuse box and carefully switched off the connection to his wing, ensuring that all his batchmates would be captive, as well as in the dark.

'Earlier that day, he had worked on the lock on a little wicket gate at the rear of the college, one that was rarely used and it took exactly seven minutes for him to get out of the compound. He ran hugging the wall and, in another ten minutes, was at the back gate of the girls' hostel. He managed to scale the gate, scraping the heel of his hand in the process.'

The old man paused and stood up, 'It is my prostrate. I have to go again.'

Vishnu was on tenterhooks waiting for the old man to return. Fifteen minutes later, he came in with the chai wallah in tow. Cups of tea were bought and paid for and the old man began to sip slowly and luxuriously, lost in thought.

'So then what happened? How did he get into the room?'

'Not so fast. He was almost caught by the chowkidar on his rounds, and had to squat among the bushes for a good half hour.

'He was bitten by mosquitoes and narrowly escaped falling into the compost pit.

'Ultimately he spotted the girl's room on the first floor. She had promised to leave it open at 1 pm and he was more than 11 hours late. Fortunately, it was still open and he clambered up the storm water pipe, scrambled on to the ledge and reached her window. By now, it was the witching hour of midnight. He heard a clock strike twelve. Just then a large bat flew very close to his face and he almost screamed and fell. He clutched wildly at the edge of the ledge and missed but caught hold of the drain pipe again. But not before his hand had slipped a few inches and a sharp piece of metal left a nasty gash in the palm of his right hand.

'With blood starting to ooze out, he got back on the ledge, pushed aside the billowing curtains and stepped into the girl's room. She was on her bed, one arm flung out almost in a dramatic gesture, looking even more beautiful in her sleep. It was a small room and she was the single occupant. Her father must have paid a lot to get his daughter a room to herself. He scurried to the table and, sure enough, there was a letter signed by her and her four friends.

'First of all, he fished out a scarf he had in his pocket and tied it around his hand to stem the flow of blood. He quickly shed his clothes, dumped them on the chair, read the letter again to make sure it was all right and shoved it into the pocket of his underpants.

'He was just about to walk out of the door and across the campus when he had an overpowering impulse to kiss her—not on her cheek but on her lips. It was part of the deal anyway, he thought, so what the hell. He went to the bed, leaned over and placed his lips against hers. Just as his senses registered that she was not warm, his eyes took in the little bottle near her hand. It was open and empty.

'The little General threw caution to the winds. His safety did not matter anymore. He had to save her. Even if he were to be severely punished or worse, even expelled, he could not just slip away. Her life suddenly became more precious than his life or his future. It was in that moment that he realized he was desperately in love and this was the woman for him. He opened the door, running down the corridor, shouting for help and banging on all the doors. Within minutes there was a gaggle of girls, gaping at a scrawny, demented figure in striped underwear blabbering something about a suicide. The warden and the resident professor joined them.

'It was the talk of the town for a long time. If it had not been for the boy, the girl would have died. She was rushed to the hospital and her stomach was pumped. She recovered and continued her studies and became a very successful psychologist…I suppose she must have worked on herself first.

'The Boy was let off with a mild warning from the principals of both colleges and was accepted as equal to the macho seniors.

In fact, he started working out and was a strapping young lad by the second year. He joined the army and retired as a Lt General.'

'But why did the girl attempt suicide?'

'That is another very long story that will need another long journey. Yes, yes, I know what you are eager to know. The boy and the girl ultimately did get married, but only after many years of friendship and separation. Now I have to get down at the next station. I am not going all the way to Delhi, you see.'

The old man got his bags together and held out his right hand.

'Wish you all the best, young man. Thank you for listening to an old man's ramblings.'

Vishnu looked down as he grasped his hand. Running vertically on the inside of the palm was a two inch scar. He looked up to see two eyes twinkling at him.

'Yes. That night did scar me forever.'

Bellow Yellow

CHINMAYI BALI

I'm the failed artist. I'm the forgotten muse. I'm the fling between the two.

Those were her last words, lazily crawled across a yellow post-it. Instead of calling the police or informing the warden and college authorities, I just sat down in her chair and tried to picture her reading them out aloud to herself after scribbling hastily. That's what she always did—rush into things and then mull over them at leisure. It was quite possible that she'd be contemplating her fatal action this very moment by posthumously narrating it to her invisible audience. The story would take on a whole new meaning in that lilting voice of hers. She'd romanticize it, paint it yellow.

I hadn't really been keen on starting college. Afraid to grow up, I ended up making a list of reasons why it wasn't a good idea to send me this far away from home. The roommate from hell topped it, of course. While I wouldn't say that she fit the description, her love of the colour yellow did make me want to throw up. I couldn't possibly live in a place that looked like a giant smiley. Also, she played Donovan's *Mellow Yellow* on a loop. I must have asked her to turn it down a zillion times but her only retort was, 'Don't you ever want to bellow yellow?' Once, I had walked into the room to find her boyfriend and her smoking dried banana skins. They sure did look wasted. The library became my home then.

I have always been a sucker for urban legends. The 'aren't you glad you didn't turn on the light?' one being my favourite. Every time I got back from the library for a book or something, I played it out in my mind. In a way, then, I had killed her many times. In more ways than one, to be honest.

If she wasn't the perfect roommate, I wasn't either. I saw her dabbing her purple bruises yellow every day and I kept quiet. She would at times play tic-tac-toe, all alone, on her forearm and I'd be blind to it. I covered up my guilt by pretending to just be another hopscotch girl. I always ignored the red splashed right in front of me. When forced to face it, I thought of perfumed hearts and evil apples. I never spoke out, never sought out any help for her.

Why even go so far back? Let me consider that morning, for instance. If only I had stayed back a little longer with her, none of this would have happened. We had a field trip scheduled for the day and I had tried waking her up in every possible way, but nothing seemed to work. Her grades had been flailing since the last semester, ever since she got involved in one of those secret projects of her good for-nothing boyfriend, and she didn't give two hoots about it. I had tried to talk her out of the relationship initially. 'Wearing only Che Guevara t-shirts does not make him one!' was my failed attempt at reasoning with her, but she brushed it off. Not only that, she then made me see the tattoo he'd made for her with cigarette burns. I cringed. 'Isn't this awesome?' she asked. I let it pass, assuming it to be a rhetorical question.

'Rise, rise, sunshine,' I mockingly sang in a matronly fashion. 'C'mon, dude! This is your one chance to get everything back on track. One silly field trip negates a thousand silly mistakes and the average goes up. Your report card will thank you for this,' I said, trying to convince her to wake up but failing miserably.

'The Sun,' she began, shading her eyes from the sunlight that streamed through the window right on her face, 'is melting as we speak. Has been melting since the beginning of the universe. It'll melt away soon into oblivion. So shall we all. You, me, those stuck-up teachers, the know-it-all first rankers—everyone!'

'Everyone except your ice queen of a boyfriend,' I said as he stormed into the room just then. His only retort was a dirty look flashed my way for a nanosecond. Surely he had other things on his mind. The moment he started calling her names, I slipped out unnoticed. I could hear him loud and clear even down the corridor. I stood there for five odd minutes, waiting for her side of the story or her accusations or her volley of beeped out flatteries, but nothing. Her soul had become used to abuse, just like her body.

I made up a quick excuse for her absence, and it didn't take me much to come up with one. While we were all waiting for the bus, my gaze kept shifting to the dorms. In a moment of frantic frenzy, I did consider going back but I restrained myself. Now I realize I shouldn't have.

Of all things, we had bonded over thanatology, and how we'd enjoy college more with that included in our curriculum. Our first and last heart to heart talk had been about death. She wanted hers to be poetic. Her suicide note makes me want to believe it was.

I twirled the yellow post-it in my hand. Refusing to let the what-ifs clog my memory, I slowly reached for the phone. I couldn't stay cooped up with her cold self for the rest of my life, anyway. It was a suicide, plain and simple, but once someone got down to the bottom of it, I would be blamed just as much as anyone who knew her would. Her masquerade of lovable eccentricities needed to be stripped the first day itself, but we all played along. Dialling the number, I knew that even yellow journalism couldn't deter me now. I had finally found the strength in me to bellow yellow.

Dare to Bare

MALATHI JAIKUMAR

Bumchik was the outcome of a 'dare'. His mother and father had been going stealthily steady for almost a year and kept tottering and teetering on the edge of a commitment. They were unable to take the plunge because of the very strong but invisible strings held firmly in the fists of their respective parents. That was until someone whispered the word 'dare' into their ears.

Shehnaz was a gentle, fair maiden who could be rightly called 'KKK' (Kashmir Ki Kali) not only because she was from Kashmir but also because she was a lot like Sharmila Tagore, dimple et al—only a lot more sharmili than the Sharmila of *An Evening in Paris*. Shiraaz was as bold as she was gentle. He was also a Kashmiri—very fair, very handsome and more prone to act than to think. In fact, he thought thinking too much was a waste of time when one could finish what was thought about in the same amount of time it took to think it through. So 'why think when you can act' was his motto.

Aided and abetted by daring friends, they eloped when both sets of parents had loosened their grips momentarily on the aforesaid strings. Eloping led to marriage, and marriage led to the inevitable result of encounters of the very close kind. Faced with the fait accompli, the parents put up a brave front and backed off from their hard stance.

Many names were suggested for the offspring in the offing, but the one that stuck for life was determined by his entry into the world. The baby refused to emerge into the world head first as all other babies abiding by the laws of nature do, and insisted on sitting on his bum inside the womb, causing much discomfort and trouble to his mother and the doctors. So it was only natural that the father, when lifting the new born in his arms, called him Bumchik.

Bumchik was even fairer than his parents and, when the full moon shone down in all its glory, he seemed to reflect the light in all its splendour. In addition to his enviable complexion that put *Fair and Lovely* to shame, he had the most innocent blue eyes, fringed by long lashes coveted by most girls. Very early on in life, his friends discovered that the words 'bet' and 'dare' touched a very deep chord in Bumchik. He responded to those words with an alacrity that equalled, and even surpassed, a well-trained champion dog's reaction to 'sit', 'heel' or 'roll over'.

As a result, in school, if someone said, 'I bet you cannot put glue on the teacher's chair,' you could be sure that Bumchik would ensure that the best glue was used to great effect in the shortest span of time. It was very fortunate that no one muttered, 'Will nobody rid me of this meddlesome priest,' within Bumchik's earshot.

So it was no surprise that Bumchik left a trail of events that were chalked up in the annals of the school's folklore—events that, though small in themselves, added up to the making of a legend. Pages in the teachers' books were mysteriously stuck together; tiffin boxes packed by loving hands turned up empty; shoelaces that revelled in their independence were suddenly entwined like Siamese twins; and crisp white shirts sprouted ink blots with gay abandon.

In spite of this spate of 'accidents', the trail led nowhere near Bumchik, who escaped scot free owing largely to the angelic expression on his much touted innocent face and his glib gift of the gab that gushed out spontaneously, conjuring up very appealing excuses. There was never any conclusive evidence and besides, the pranks he undertook were never hurtful or demeaning. They merely provided a good laugh, although some of the victims may not have seen the funny side. As a gesture of goodwill, Bumchik periodically played a joke on himself so that others could laugh at his expense—like the time he pinned a note on the back of his own shirt and pretended not to know why others sniggered around him.

By the time he graduated out of school, he had left behind a legion of students and teachers who thought life would be much duller on the campus without Bumchik bumming around. But the school's loss was the college's gain. His fame had gone ahead of him and he could not afford to slacken with a reputation to preserve. Without faltering or losing pace, he carried the same verve and audacity into the larger campus of the college. In fact, he viewed the school and college campus at par with the campus of life, with the result that his vision grew wider and more comprehensive.

There were many accomplishments to his credit, although most, if not all, episodes were declared as 'closed cases' with no conclusive investigation or conviction. A professor's cycle was found halfway up the steeple, defying imagination and gravity. It has still not been discovered how that feat was achieved successfully or by whom. Another rather pompous gentleman was surprised to see a letter to the editor in his name in one of the most widely circulated newspapers, describing the glories of a celestial object on a certain night at 11 pm. He was even more taken aback to see an equally ecstatic letter echoing his sentiments about the UFO the next day, signed by a maiden he secretly adored from afar. But the one and only story that is still told and retold around campfires and at midnight revelries is the day Bumchik dared to bare.

Every college campus has its share of 'khadoos' and

'moosoodoos'. For the uninitiated, both words, one in Hindi and the other in Tamil, mean the same—grumpy and devoid of all humour. Mr Sharma, or Sharmaji as he was called, taught Hindi most seriously, and he took himself even more seriously. When God sculpted his features, He probably started with a pig in mind and, being diverted by some emergency, ended with a fish. As a result, while the eyes and the nose immediately took you back to Porky Pig, the mouth with its downturn was definitely fishy. No one had ever seen Sharmaji smile and the only expression reflected on his face was very much akin to that of a person who had just caught a strong whiff of some foul odour from the drain.

The origin of the bet has faded over the murky years, but it is a fact that Bumchik was offered a hundred bucks to knock on Sharmaji's door in the dead of night and bare himself in all his pristine fairness. There was no risk of anyone else but Sharmaji opening the door as he was a bachelor living in single blessedness— not very surprising as he was yet to meet his match in grumpiness.

On the appointed full moon night, just before the clock struck twelve, Bumchik stepped out, wrapped in nothing more than a white bed sheet. He padded across to the faculty residence, walked confidently up to the door of Sharmaji's house and knocked with great aplomb.

There was no immediate response, which necessitated another knock, this time a little bit louder. A few minutes later, he heard the latch being pulled and the door opened—first a crack, then half open, and finally, fully open. Bumchik, aware that no one would throw his door wide open at that time of night, had cleverly stepped aside after knocking, forcing Sharmaji to almost come out and look around. At that very moment, he dramatically whipped the sheet off, holding the ends in his two outspread hands in a very good imitation of the stance on the prow of the Titanic. The full moon cloaked his naked body in silvery white. For one brief moment, Sharmaji looked fishier with his mouth open. Before he could recover from or react to the apparition before him, Bumchik had folded his arms and, consequently, the sheet around him and made a speedy exit.

Back with his friends, he collected the wager with due grace and accepted the applause with as much modesty as a man most immodestly dressed (or undressed) could muster. They would have all gone to bed satisfied with a good night's work had someone not piped up to offer double the amount for an encore.

By now, half an hour had elapsed and Bumchik set out again on his mission. This time, the door opened at the first knock and Bumchik had to rely on his very quick reflexes to spread his arms wide and offer just a glimpse of his luminous beauty before beating a very hasty retreat. It all took place so fast that Sharmaji did not even have the time to blink.

Excitement ran high and the group of boys doubled up with laughter at the very thought of Sharmaji's face. It was a unanimous decision that there had to be one last curtain call to the act—with a higher wager, of course! There were a few who sounded a note of caution, but they were silenced quickly and effectively.

By now the moon rode high over the campus, bathing the whole ground in a bright white light. Bumchik walked with well-practiced ease to run through his act. This time, the door opened with great alacrity and Sharmaji, who had been waiting with a stick in hand, rushed out with a roar. Bumchik, who valued his health more than his nakedness, let the sheet fall and took to his heels. He ran with his long hair and other small parts of his body flailing as he put distance between himself and his pursuer. They must have run a couple of times around the complex with Sharmaji puffing and panting, losing ground steadily until, unable to keep up with the nimble youngster, he slowed down to a walk. He decided to check each and every student's room, knowing that it would be next to impossible to hide a large Kashmiri in the raw.

Bumchik, meanwhile, ran to the hostel and raced up the stairs to his room. He quickly put on his pyjamas, was joined by a few friends and they all sat around the table with books opened in front of them. Ten minutes later, when Sharmaji came to inspect all the rooms, he found a very studious group in Bumchik's room, burning the midnight oil. All the students swore that they had been studying for the past hour or more and had not stirred. They vouched for Bumchik's presence as well and insisted that Sharmaji had been hallucinating.

Ever since that day, there was always a mildly unbelieving and speculative look on Sharmaji's face whenever his glance fell on Bumchik. This was followed by barely audible chuckles and laughter that rustled through the students as they occupied themselves busily with various tasks that had suddenly assumed great importance. Only Bumchik seemed completely at ease, his blue-eyed gaze fixed steadily on Sharmaji.

Sharmaji blinked.

Fresher

SNEH THAKUR

I stood surrounded by a group of angry, spiteful faces.

Tyagi 'Sir' was shaking an accusing finger at me, screaming, 'Tell us! Tell us who gave you this CD or you will face the consequences.'

Consequences.

I looked at him, closed my eyes, and thought about what I was going to say.

I came to Indore eight months ago. Most girls from cities like Delhi never venture out, at least not to smaller towns like Indore. Most of them don't need to, if you survive the almost inhumane minimum percentages that are put forth as eligibility criteria each year. But that was never the problem with me. I was an adventurous soul who wanted to make it to whichever college chose me on my merit, with one condition—it had to be a college outside Delhi. I thought that to succeed in life, I had to learn how to live without my silver spoon—namely, the car and driver and the cushy home that had every amenity under the sun.

I wanted to get away from home and experience something new, something exciting, something life-changing. I applied to every medical college there was outside Delhi—far-flung places in Karnataka, Tamil Nadu and Madhya Pradesh, and finally, I made it to a city in the heart of India—Indore. The pre-medical entrance exam was harder than I had expected. Luckily for me, my strategy of studying one subject better than the others worked and I made it on most of the biology questions. I even got a top 5 ranking for the first time in over 18 entrance tests. Beat that!

Mom and Dad were not happy with my decision to move to Indore. They said it was too far away from them and that no one they knew had ever sent their daughters there to study. The more they said this, the more it reinforced my decision. This was it. My chance to experience something which was not pre-selected or pre-meditated. It was going to be my choice. I felt the joy that only true freedom can bring. It was to be short-lived.

I didn't introduce myself to Indore too well. Or so it seemed. The first day of college, I put on my best pair of clothes—a nice FIFA T-shirt, cargo pants (the latest trend that season) and a pair of blue and white sneakers. I had even washed my hair the night before to avoid any last minute chance of a bad hair day. I walked into college with a bounce in my step, my hair bouncing along with my happy footsteps.

'Eyy… You.'

I turned around to face the person who addressed me in, well, such a ridiculous manner.

Tyagi, they called him. I later learnt that he was a fourth year senior from a town called Bhilai in Madhya Pradesh. He had flunked the medical exams two years in a row, thus making him 'the most senior of the seniors'.

Great, I thought. Lady Luck seemed to have something in store for me on the very first day of college.

'Yes?' I said, cautiously approaching Tyagi 'Sir' who was what can only be described as 'lounging on the footsteps of the temple of education'.

I felt Tyagi's eyes do a biometric body scan of me. Why did they need to teach Radiology as a subject in this college? They should just hire this fellow, I thought.

'New Girl?'

No, you dodo. Not 'New Girl'. Do I seem like an infant to you?

'Yes.'

He chews on something, a paan probably, given his stained lips, which are now beginning to reveal themselves as he grins at me.

'Accha, where from you?'

'Delhi... And you are?' I say, now visibly irritated at this.

'*Tumhara baap*,' he answers.

There is a sudden echo of laughter and I think I might be imagining it so look behind me. Like a group of vultures who have just found a juicy carcass, I find a group of people have gathered behind me, a strange look of satisfaction on their faces.

'I am late for class,' I say, adjusting my bag and taking a step towards the college main door.

'Seniors. You know names?' asks Tyagi, pointing a finger at the people standing behind me.

I look at them and think to myself, No, and I wouldn't care.

'I am sure it will be a pleasure to get to know all of you, but for now, I am late for class.' I shift the strap of my bag to my right shoulder and walk away, weaving my way through the seniors behind me. I catch a glimpse of Tyagi who has a look of alarm on his face, as though told that he would have to repeat yet another year.

The days that followed were even worse. As 'juniors', we were expected to do some ridiculous things, like having our hair covered in oil when we came to college, wearing chappals instead of shoes, and salwar suits with V-shaped dupattas pinned on either side. Luckily for me, I had a sense of fashion. So I managed hairdos which looked chic even though slick with oil. I wore dupattas in interesting ways even though pinned on the side. This seemed to frustrate my seniors who could not find anything 'technically incorrect' with my creative renditions. During our introduction sessions, we were expected to introduce ourselves and our hobbies in 'shudh Hindi'. I found these exercises ridiculous but learnt to say things like 'surfing the internet' in Hindi. Overall, I took it as a necessary and harmless exercise and so, went along with it, even enjoying myself, to the frustration of Tyagi who was present at all the 'introduction' sessions. As juniors, we were told to address our seniors with a 'Ma'am' or a 'Sir'. But I never did that, saving it for my professors at college. Tyagi was most irked by this and made it evident by calling me 'Madam' in a mocking way every time he saw me. My batchmates tried to warn me to fall in line, saying that Tyagi was connected with the Indore underworld and that there was a rumour he had even been to jail once. I stuck to my views on not addressing my seniors as 'Sir' and 'Ma'am', as I found it unnecessary and believed that those titles were earned and not threatened out of people.

On Friday nights, we had 'hostel calls'. It was as shady an experience as it sounded. Twenty-four of my batch mates and I would have to turn up at 9 pm sharp at Vidhya 'Ma'am's' room. There, we would be asked to stand in a line, height wise and close, so that all our bottoms would be aligned as well as they possibly could be. We would spend about twenty minutes getting it just right, and then the chants would begin.

'*Chaaawani…Athannii…*'

'*Chawani, Athani, Athani, Chawani…*'

Chawani meant that all of us would have to thrust our hips to the right (also called a thumka in Hindi), and Athani meant to the left. Depending on the tone, speed and flair with which Vidhya 'Ma'am' would sing out these words, we would have to comply, thus bringing new meaning to the phrase 'making one dance to someone else's tunes'. After about an hour of this, we would be asked to face backwards and continue doing the same, now with our bottoms facing our amused seniors. I have yet to comprehend what they found so amusing about so many wobbly bottoms. But to each his own.

Some of the seniors had begun to like me, or so it seemed. Vikram, a second year senior, approached me after one of the 'introduction' sessions.

'So how are you finding it here now?' he asked.

'I am looking forward to our Freshers' party. All the juniors are thinking of which chappals will look good at a disco,' I said smiling. Vikram laughed.

The Freshers' party was the 'coming of age' party after six months of 'introduction' sessions. It was the party in which titles like 'Miss Fresher' and 'Mr Fresher' were handed out, based on an 'intelligent assessment of each junior and their potential'. I was just looking forward to it so that I could go to college the next day wearing my normal clothes and shoes.

'Best of luck for that!' Vikram said, winked at me and then walked away.

In the following months, Vikram introduced me to the rest of his gang. There was Mohit, the aspiring model who was stuck at medical college for some reason that was not very clear to me. There was Shweta, the obese and insecure one who kept looking at me like I was some intrusion in her life, clearly hating the attention that I now seemed to be getting. And, of course, Priya, the 'modern' straight-talking size-zero wannabe and Miss Fresher at their batch's Freshers' party. The party may have been two years back, but the title seemed to be stuck forever like a bubble around her head. Even though Vikram's gang seemed like nice people, I found the attention and respect they gave Tyagi (in doses of 'Sir' suffixed to everything addressed to him) a bit odd. I attributed this to the need to survive and ignored the thought.

In August, it had been six months and the Freshers' party was organised in the discotheque of Indore's best hotel, Sayaji. The party was mildly enjoyable. I had never danced to so many Hindi tracks from the 1980s before. I found myself the centre of attention with most of the male seniors flocking around me for a dance. So it came as a bit of a surprise when my roommate Vrinda, and not I, won the Miss Fresher title. Vrinda was a pretty Punjabi girl from Delhi, and I later learnt that Mohit, the aspiring model who was the judge of the competition, had a special place in his heart for her. It seemed that she reciprocated as well, as they shared the last dance of the evening to 'Kuch Na Kaho…Kuch Bhi Na Kaho' as a slow dance by the blaring speakers.

After the Freshers' party, life seemed to return to normal. I was back to wearing my cargo pants and sleeveless shirts. I found it flattering when only a week after my debut as a non-oiled, shoe-wearing person, a majority of my female seniors had magically found their cargo pants too and now roamed around college like clones.

It was Independence Day when it happened.

I was walking past the library when Vikram came running towards me.

Catching his breath, he said, 'Can you do me favour? I need to get these CDs and books to Priya at the hostel. Can you give them to her?'

'Sure!' I said. 'I was just going back to the hostel anyway.'

I took the wrapped packet from Vikram and smiled.

'You're welcome, by the way!' I said grinning. Vikram smiled and then sprinted off to what seemed to be a class he was late for again.

I took the Suar Bhat, Indore's very own noisy contraption of a public transport vehicle, to the hostel. The hostel was usually quiet at this time of the day as most of the students were still getting back from a day at college.

I approached room number 12 on the first floor. The first floor was mostly occupied by seniors, some sort of a tribute to their seniority—the gift of climbing a lesser number of stairs.

I knocked on a door full of stickers and said, 'Priya, I have a parcel for you from Vikram.'

'Come in!' she yelled from inside.

Priya was sitting in a tank top and shorts having lunch, 'Ah… Thanks! Would you like some lunch?'

'No thanks, I'll just run along. I have another class at 6.' I waved goodbye and went to my room for a power nap before my class.

I woke up about twenty minutes later to the sound of loud banging on my door.

'Open the door! Open the door!'

I opened the door, rubbing my eyes groggily.

'How dare you!' yelled Priya. Her voice echoed through the hall, making many of my batchmates come out of their rooms.

'What?' I asked, not comprehending.

'How dare you! What sort of a girl do you think I am?'

'I do not understand. What happened?' I asked, now fully awake.

'Do you have no shame giving me CDs with porn? What sort of a girl are you?' By now, the entire hostel had come out to witness the source of the screaming.

'But Priya, I was only delivering a parcel from Vikram…' I said, shocked.

'Don't you lie! He never gave you this. I asked him,' she said, fuming.

'What? No, that's not right. I'm not lying!' I said, trying to convince her.

'We'll see you in college,' she said and then stormed out.

I got ready for college in a daze. How could this be happening?

What did this mean? Why did Vikram deny handing me the parcel? Was it some sort of a mistake? What did Priya mean by, 'We'll see you in college'? Would she inform the Director? Oh boy, what kind of trouble I was in!

I took the Suar Bhat back to college and, for once, its noise was a welcome distraction from my thoughts. I walked towards the college main door with a frown on my face, thinking that I had to get Vikram and Priya together and sort out the misunderstanding.

I opened the door to my classroom.

My batchmates were seated on their respective seats. Surrounding them were my seniors. Second year, third year, fourth year students…and Tyagi.

'Ah, look who is here! Miss Delhi!' said Tyagi mockingly. 'Come, come…We are all waiting for you only.'

I walked confused towards my seat and placed my bag down. A sort of a semi-circle had formed around me and I began to get very uncomfortable.

'So, Delhi Girl, want to explain?' said Tyagi, his paan-stained lips smirking at me.

'Explain what?' I said, still standing.

'You have the balls to give porn to your senior? Is this what they teach you in Delhi?' he said in a booming voice. Vrinda looked at me accusingly as though I had committed some kind of sin. The rest of my batchmates were either shaking their heads or whispering amongst themselves.

'You think you are some kind of especial girl, huh? Miss Fresher or something?' said Tyagi, looking around. The seniors around us started laughing.

'And you lie also! Wah wah! Saying bad things about your seniors who are nice to you?' said Tyagi, looking over to his right.

To his right were Shweta, a disgusted look on her face, Mohit,

Priya and Vikram. I looked over to Vikram with the hope that he would clarify things. I noticed his arm around Priya's shoulders. Priya pretended to be suitably distressed and loved the attention she was getting.

'I did not lie. I was asked to deliver the parcel to Priya,' I said, clearing my throat. My voice sounded a bit nervous. My mind was trying to process everything. This was ridiculous. Why was this meeting called? How did Priya get here so fast and why did she get everyone involved? Why was it considered a matter of 'public interest'?

'So now you are saying you got a parcel from someone and you did not know? You deliver things like this? So there must be a especial arrangement with this person, a?' Tyagi mocked, winking at those around him.

I looked at Vikram, appalled at what was happening. And then, I noticed the smirk on his face. It all fell into place. The faked niceness. The hidden motives. Their friendship with Tyagi.

From the very first day when I walked in, I had disregarded Tyagi. I never called him 'Sir' like the rest of the bunch. I wore what I wanted to, was never intimidated by him, never did the assignments which he tried to pass on to me, and never became overtly friendly with any of my seniors. And now, this was their way of putting me in my place.

I stood surrounded by a group of angry, spiteful faces.

Tyagi 'Sir' was shaking an accusing finger at me, 'Tell us! Tell us who gave you this CD, or you will face the consequences.'

Consequences.

I looked at him, closed my eyes, and thought about what I was going to say.

'I am never going to tell you who gave this to me.'

I got into my seat and placed my bag on the desk. And smiled.

Looking Back

Strangers in Strange Places

ABHIJIT BHADURI

What is it about alumni meets that transcends geographies and timelines? We all believe we went to this great place and had a fun time in school/college/B-School/Med School...You get the drift. Whenever we talk about our college days and college friends there is an entire piece of nostalgia that inevitably wipes off every piece of unpleasant reality of those golden days. I got bullied in school because I was fat (make that description present continuous) and got horrible grades. College and B-School were no different. Everyone hated me. I had no friends. Yet when you meet a classmate many years later, they seem to treat you like a long lost cousin. Isn't that strange?

I remember once bumping into Pingala Reddy, my classmate from school. It was a cold winter evening in December and a freak snowstorm had made it impossible for me to get a cab to the airport in that one-horse town, a few hundred miles from Chicago. When I reached the airport I was horribly late and had missed the last flight to civilization. The ground staff at the airport was packing up to go home and were in no mood to practise 'Customer is King'. I tried to explain to the obese bored woman at the counter how important it was for me to get that flight, failing which the solution to global hunger would be delayed. Global hunger still remains an issue—and yes, I did miss my flight.

I turned back to see a fat and balding man in a trenchcoat

smiling at my agony. I was about to give him a piece of my mind when he said, 'Abbey, what the hell are you doing here?'

'I am trying to board this flight and do you mind standing in queue and waiting for your turn?'

'I live here, you moron.'

Well, I thought, you are the one who lives here in the back of beyond. So how does that make me a moron?

'Aren't you Pingy…Er…I mean, aren't you Pingala Reddy? I wouldn't have recognized you. This is crazy. I am stuck here until tomorrow afternoon. Excuse me, but I need to find a cab to take me to the hotel. This place has only 2 cabs, I think, and one just left.'

'You are wrong. Both have left. Just pick up your bags and come over to my home. My wife and kids would love to meet you.'

The choice was between spending the night at the airport and staying with Pingy. I opted for the tougher choice. I hesitated simply because, even though he had been my classmate in school, we had barely exchanged a few sentences during our twelve years together.

Pingy introduced me to his American wife, Kathy, and his son, Josh, who was into baseball and wrestling! When you have a snowstorm brewing outside, being indoors next to the fireside is the closest to heaven you can get. Pingy and Kathy were gracious hosts and went out of their way to make me feel comfortable. Josh explained how Graeco-Roman wrestling was the toughest because holds are allowed only above the waist. He would have taught me more, but Pingy sent him off on an errand. Fifteen minutes later, Pingy and I were sampling the contents of his bar and chatting about our school days. It was an animated conversation. We talked about all the classmates we were in touch with. He was interesting company. I wondered why everyone disliked him so much in school. Nobody wanted to be known as Pingy's friend. Even someone like me, who had no friends, resisted the temptation of inviting Pingy to my birthday party. Eventually, for want of a guest list, I had to stop celebrating my birthday.

When I jog my memory I just remember Pingy as the fat, rich kid who was inevitably given time off during music lessons. The music teacher had summoned enough courage to tell Pingy's parents (who doted on him) that there was not a single note out of the seven that he could ever sing. We laughed loudly as I narrated the incident when Suhail Akhtar had brought a field mouse to school.

I discovered Supreet Madan was now an investment banker, that Sonny Rebello was a chef at the New York Palace Hotel and that Mayank Kapoor had become a hotshot civil servant and was a part of the Prime Minister's secretariat. Wow! We were suitably inebriated when we finished talking about everyone in school and the cute girl Jasmine whom everyone had loved.

The next afternoon, Pingy dropped me off at the airport (he had taken a day off). Was he so friendly to me because he had no friends even there? I don't know. Maybe I was just a paranoid man who would never have friends anywhere. Maybe we were more inclined to be kind to each other now that we had matured as adults. Would the relationship have been the same if we were colleagues in the same firm? I wonder. Could it be that in strange places even strangers become friends?

Time

AHMED FAIYAZ

Vijay Kashyap strode into the clinic looking relaxed. After his retirement from the hospital, he had slowed down in more ways than one. He had decided to come and volunteer at the clinic run by an NGO his wife supported, that served the underprivileged in the neighbourhood. Although he came in for two hours each evening, it was a very different setting from what he had been used to in over thirty years of practice at Get Well Hospital. Patients would line up at his door on seeing him enter, and sometimes fight to go ahead and see the good doctor. He often ended up seeing forty to fifty patients a day, most complaining of the usual flu, mild food poisoning, and minor cuts and burns. Two hours often extended to three, and Dr Kashyap didn't mind as it was his way of giving back to the community.

He still had a regular stream of patients who visited him in the morning at a small clinic in his backyard. With a cardiologist son in London, another a software engineer in California, and with over thirty years of practice, he didn't really need the money.

After a long evening, he began to pack up his little case and was about to head out for his evening walk at a park nearby when the usually reticent nurse stepped in his path.

'Doctor Sir, if you don't mind…There is one more patient, Mrs Matthew. She has come from far away and has been waiting for you,' she said, looking at him hopefully.

'Hmm...Why didn't you say so earlier? Can she not come back tomorrow? What's the matter?' he asked, looking at her worried expression.

'Actually, she's an old teacher, Doctor. She lives in the same quarters as us. Her husband, who was a constable, passed away twenty years ago. He was a drunkard, a very troublesome man. She's got a son in the Gulf but he...'

'Listen, I don't want her life story. What's the matter with her? You obviously know this woman, Mala...'

'Yes Doctor, a very good lady, like my mother. She has a lot of pain in her knee. She can't sit down, cannot bend her knee.'

'How old is she?'

'She's about 72, Doctor. Here is her X-ray report. I arranged to get it diagnosed. My sister works at the lab...'

Dr Kashyap took the big white envelope from her and removed the X-ray. He studied it carefully and shook his head in dismay. 'Maybe four or five years ago, it would have been easier. Her kneecap is completely worn out. She needs knee replacement surgery, which is very expensive. Given what you say about her, she'll have to live with it. What can I do, Mala? I can treat patients here for minor ailments. I prescribe medications that the dispensary provides at a subsidized rate. With this case, I can't do much. I'm a physician, not an orthopaedist,' he said, shrugging his shoulders, and started to walk towards the door.

'Doctor, please see her for five minutes. She's under a lot of pain! She came here with great difficulty,' Mala pleaded.

'Okay, send her in,' he said and sat back in his chair staring at the X-ray. Her knee was damaged beyond repair.

He nodded at her without looking up, as she wished him good evening and walked slowly into the consultation room.

'Yes, I've seen your report...' he stopped for a moment,

surprised by what he saw. It was who he thought she was. She looked frail and worn, a pale shadow of the person she once was, her beauty now ravaged by the sands of time and her apparent misfortune over the decades. She wore a pale old salwar kameez and had a head full of grey hair. 'I will recommend you to my colleague, Dr Shukla, at Get Well Hospital. He should be able to do the surgery…'

'But Doctor, I'm a very poor woman. I can't pay for all this. Can you give me some medicine to suppress the pain?' she looked at him with her kind eyes, in the same way she had decades ago. Only this time, he saw pain and helplessness in them.

'See Mrs Matthews, the NGO will take care of all the expenses, not to worry. In the budget, there are certain cases that we can support and you are definitely someone we want to help,' he said, leaning in and smiling at her. She, of course, didn't recognize him. He was fat, bald and almost three times the size than when she had last seen him, forty-seven years ago.

'Thank you, Doctor! God bless you and your family…' Hot tears ran down her cheeks and she wiped her face with her dull dupatta.'

'Nahin madam, I'm glad to be of assistance,' he said awkwardly, returning her smile. His heart beat faster than normal and he quickly wrote her a prescription.

'I'm prescribing some painkillers for you. Please take these and call me tomorrow. I'll let you know when we can meet at the hospital and I'll hand over your case to Dr Shukla.'

'Thank you,' she said, smiling faintly as she took the prescription from his thick hands, and he averted his gaze from hers.

'Thank you, Doctor!' Mala said, running into the room a few minutes later while he sat with his hand on his chin and his thoughts far away.

'Don't worry, I'll take care of it and see that she gets better. She seems wonderful,' he said beaming at her.

Mala almost rushed to hug him, but contained herself. She turned around and left the room.

He took out his phone and dialled a number. 'Shukla, yes it's me... Radha is okay... Yes, listen, I had a favour to ask of you... There is this lady who needs a knee replacement... She's come through someone close... Yes, I'll pay... If you can waive your fee... Consider it for me... A very special case... Yes... You will... That's wonderful, thank you... Alright then... No, I'll bring her myself,' he said before hanging up.

♦

Vijay pulled out another bit of chapatti from his box and dipped it into the curry. He looked up to see Ms Sheila stand before him with a frown on her face. *Why is she looking at me like that? I don't trouble her at all.* He, in fact, sat a short distance from the staff room where Ms Sheila ate lunch every day. He waited for the lunch break to catch a glimpse of her. Her, with her slender frame, silky long hair, kohl in her dark brown eyes and a beauty spot near her upper lip. He gaped at her with devotion every morning in class, without any attention paid to what she was teaching. She was fourteen years older than him, but that didn't matter. He worshipped her like a lot of the other guys did, probably a little more.

'Good afternoon... M-M-Miss,' he said nervously.

'What's going on with you, Vijay?' she asked with her hand on her hip.

'Miss?' he said, looking like a lovesick puppy.

'Your grades are slipping in all subjects. Ms Rita says you've failed in Maths this term. Many teachers complain that you're inattentive…Why isn't your focus on your books? You know how hard your mother has to work…' She knew all about his humble background and his family's struggles.

'I can't really understand what Ms Rita does in geometry class, Miss.' This was only partly true, as his mind was on Ms Sheila half the time. 'I can't afford tuition fees like the other boys.'

'I know all the geometry you need to be taught. You bring your books and come over to the staff room for a few minutes after school every day. You can ask me doubts, not just in geometry, but anything else…' 'Thank you Miss!' he said, looking up at her and smiling.

'I want you to help your family out of a difficult existence. You need to work hard, promise me,' she said firmly.

'Yes Miss,' he promised, his cheeks flushed with embarrassment.

'Run along now. I see you sitting here alone every day. Finish your lunch and go play with the other students in the field.'

He nodded and looked down at his lunchbox. He lived up to his promise, focusing on his studies, and his grades constantly improved. Sheila tutored him every day for an hour, helping him with problems and advising him on how to prepare. Every day, they walked together after school to the bus stop. She took the 92A at 4 p.m., and he the 98E at 4.15. He stood third in class at the end of the year. It was a memorable day when she excitedly ruffled his hair and kissed him on his cheek with pride in her eyes. 'You'll become someone successful in life!' she gushed. 'Keep working hard!' At the end of the year, during the summer holidays, she married a young constable and left the city never to return.

◆

Dr Kashyap walked home in a sullen mood, feeling devastated

about the state that she was in. There was a time when he had loved her. He had yearned for her acceptance, and praise from her mouth had meant the world to him. He had lived up to her expectations and succeeded in life. He pondered over the many times he had hoped to meet her. She would have been proud to see him graduate through medical school, forty years ago. He had imagined her sitting and watching his graduation ceremony. He had wished she were at his wedding, at the time he was made the Head of Department, fifteen years ago. But here she was—alone, helpless and broken. *I'll take care of her. I will,* he told himself as he opened the gate and walked into his bungalow.

Remember Me?

AHMED FAIYAZ

'Damn, bro! Do you see that girl? Black dress, long hair, at nine o'clock,' Ajit said to Sudeep at the bar. It was the after-party for the launch of a fashion brand, at Henry's Shack in Lower Parel.

'Wow! She is bloody hot. Is she some long lost cousin? Tell me she is!' Sudeep said, pushing back his gelled hair and taking a swig from his pint of beer as he fixed his gaze on a group of friends, which the beautiful girl having a drink was a part of.

'Are you nuts? She is Ruheen, man…Ruheen Oberoi! She was a popular girl back at Lawrence Girls. She once had a crush on me,' Ajit said like an excited schoolboy, rolling up the sleeves of his maroon party shirt.

Sudeep looked at him and snickered. He was round and short with a receding hairline and more hair on his face than on his head—certainly didn't figure as someone the most gorgeous girl in the room would have a crush on.

'Sure!'

'She was, man! I'm telling you.'

'Come on dude, nice one. The joke is over. Find a less gorgeous woman and maybe then I'll consider believing you. She's way out of your league, man.'

'Oh yeah? You think I'm fibbing. Man, I was on the cricket and football teams both. I also held the record for the 100 metre sprint for three years. Those days were different. I'm just a little out of shape now.' He tucked his beer belly in and ran his palm over his paunch.

'A little?'

'Yeah, put a lid on it,' he said with irritation.

'The woman who had a crush on you is walking up to the bar,' Sudeep said with raised eyebrows. 'Let's see if she remembers you.'

'Two mojitos please,' she said to the bartender, within their earshot. She turned with a polite smile to look at the guys who couldn't stop staring at her. As she waited, Ajit crept up to her.

'Hi,' he said with a wide grin.

'Hi,' she said with little interest, and turned around to look at her friends.

'You don't remember me. You're Ruheen, right? From Lawrence Girls?' He stood before her with one hand in his pocket, and in the other he held his pint of beer.

'That's right,' she said with a friendly smile. 'I'm sorry, do I know you?'

'Ajit,' he said proudly. 'Vice President, Corporate Banking at Royal Bank of Ireland.' He quickly dug out a card and handed it to her.

'Ajit?'

'Yes, from Lawrence Boys. I was a year senior to you. I was on the cricket and football team. I remember you cheering me on from the side lines,' he said, with a slight smile. Sudeep looked on with a grin, clearly enjoying this conversation.

'Sorry, school is a bit of a haze for me. It seems so long ago,' she said, putting her hand on her forehead. He was clearly smitten by her presence. Half the guys at the bar had their eyes on her. The other half were too drunk to care.

'You really don't remember?' Ajit said, fixing his gaze on her beautiful eyes.

'Maybe you can jog my memory a bit,' she said sportingly.

'Well, back in those days, you had a crush on me,' he said putting on hand on his chest, while she looked at him with laughter in her eyes.

'Really?'

'Yes, you gave me a card on Valentine's Day. I was dating your senior, Mukta Bakshi, back when we knew each other. You even came up a week later and said that you really liked me. We were playing against Mayo College and you came to cheer us on,' he said. He appeared short of breath and began to sweat.

'No, sorry! Doesn't ring a bell. My fault, bad memory,' she said, turning her gaze to look at Sudeep, who was finding it hard to contain his laughter.

'How about we start from the beginning? Do you want to have a drink with us?' he asked as she turned to look in the direction of her friends again. The bartender pushed two mojitos across the table.

'Thanks, but I got my drink,' she said, picking up her glass. 'I better head back, my boyfriend is waiting for his drink. It was nice chatting with you Ajay,' she said with a cordial smile. 'You know, if I liked you that much, I'd remember you,' she preened.

'It's Ajit,' he said feebly, but she had started to walk away already.

He turned around to look at Sudeep who had a wide grin plastered on his face. 'Chal Ajay, finish your drink. Let's go,' he said.

'Screw you! At least she remembered me...Sort of. I told you she was from my school. I can't believe she's denying...'

'Oh c'mon, man. Maybe you have her mixed up with someone else. Nice try!' Sudeep said, patting his back, while Ajit sat on the barstool with his head down and sipped on his beer.

◆

'How did it go, Ruhi?' Aditya asked with a grin, as Ruheen handed him a drink.

'Of course he remembers me. He wanted me to join him for a drink. He's a VP in some bank now,' she smiled.

'Nice, did you remember him?' Aditya smirked.

'No I didn't. He was almost pleading back there, reminding me that I had a crush on him, about how I came and gave him a card etc.'

'Ha ha, sounds like it was fun. What did you say?'

'Said I didn't remember at all, Adi. That I would have if I really liked him.'

'Wicked girl.'

'Right! He went and gloated about my card to the whole world. His collar went up. He went around showing off, feeling like a stud Ruheen Oberoi had a crush on. Wonder what I saw in him,' she said, finishing her drink quickly.

'Hmm ... I know,' he smiled sheepishly. 'That's why you insisted on going up to the bar to get us drinks.'

'Yeah huh, he couldn't stop gaping at me, and possibly boasting about his glory days to his friend at the bar. Thought that I'd set him right,' she said gingerly.

'I'm sure his buddy thinks he's an ass now. You're done being mischievous for the night?'

'No sweetie, not yet,' she cooed. She noticed Sudeep still had his eyes on her.

She pulled Aditya closer to her and kissed him full on his lips. He took her hand and they walked out of the lounge a minute later. She tossed Ajit's card in the trash before she got into the car with Aditya and sped away.

●

'Dude. See, your Ruheen is leaving with the guy she just made out with,' Sudeep said, tapping on Ajit's shoulder with a smirk on his face.

'Let it be, man. Time to go home,' Ajit said, looking crestfallen and setting down his empty bottle of beer. He stood up and quietly headed towards the exit.

You can read about Ruheen and Aditya's love and relationship in *Another Chance*, the contemporary love saga of a generation. Now available at an MRP of ₹295 at bookstores nationwide.

An Accidental Start

KUNAL DHABALIA

Professor Mitra put down his pen and rubbed his eyes. He stood up and the chair almost toppled over. He had a weird equation with chairs—they kept falling over whenever he was around. Something to do with centre of gravity, he had once heard the Physics professor try to explain. *Leave Physics, it is time for English,* he thought. Straightening his back, he turned towards the clock and saw that it was an hour past midnight. He had been checking the mid-year English examination papers for nearly four hours now and one paper was still left. His tired eyes wanted respite, but he had procrastinated long enough. He had to submit the scores the next afternoon, and thus the answer sheet of roll number 64 found its way to Professor Mitra's hands.

A sigh escaped his lips when he saw the long answers scribbled on the answer sheet, and the four attached supplement sheets. He decided to skim through the answers instead of reading them completely. *I deserve a break,* he thought and started reading the initial couple of lines before scoring any answer. After checking the first three answers in a similar manner, he felt guilty. He knew it was not right; taking a shortcut was not the way he usually did things. He was generally very meticulous. He started reading the complete answers, in spite of knowing that he would have to be awake for at least another hour. He had no inkling that he would be awake till the wee hours of morning, staring at the answer sheet.

The answer to the question, 'What did the protagonists of *Damaged Goods* do on New Year's Eve that they regretted later on, and how did this impact their subsequent actions?' started innocuously with the first two lines stating a few basic facts about the story, and then it veered to something completely bizarre. Roll number 64 had taken the protagonists of the story in question and had woven a small scene around them. This had beefed up the answer, and as roll number 64 had used all the key components mentioned in the question—the characters, the setting of the story, and the mood of the scene—a casual glance would determine that the answer indeed seemed proper. The red pen scribbled out the 3 marked earlier, and scored 0.

Professor Mitra moved to the next question, 'In the monologue towards the end of *Shuttered Paradise*, explain the figures of speech used.' The answer had started with, 'He thought, in his thoughts he worded his sentences, he added similes and metaphors, phrases and idioms flowed, in his thoughts he read the prose, rewording it, rephrasing it...' On his first reading, the professor had picked up the keywords and given roll number 64 a score of four. This time he read ahead, 'Words deserted him in a surfeit of thoughts. He had a hundred and twenty thoughts, but words were none. The more he thought, the less he wrote. Enough, he said, and stopped thinking. He shut the door, and peeped out at every thought that knocked, refusing entry to all but one. The cacophony subsided, and a soulful rendering filled the room.'

His pen hovered over the score, waiting to scratch it out, but he had enjoyed reading the two answers the student had written. He debated with himself about his next line of action and reluctantly put his pen down. He read the complete answer sheet and the four attached supplements end to end and felt refreshed. He felt as if he had just finished reading a breezy story written by Wodehouse.

With every answer the protagonists had changed, the scenes had changed—what had not changed was the complete mastery over the English language. Roll number 64 had toyed with words, played with emotions, and with each answer had come up with an engrossing read.

When Professor Mitra finally put down the paper, the clock was about to strike the gong four times. His body was tired, but sleep was miles away. He was facing a moral dilemma. If he scored this paper normally, as he would with any English exam, roll number 64 was not even getting a score of 20 out of 100. But then the student had displayed that he did have good command over the language. This decision was not going to be easy. He wished he had the liberty of using a third umpire. He smiled at his own pathetic attempt at humour and decided on the most obvious course of action—procrastination. He left the decision for the next morning.

♦

Sitting on the last bench, Vikram was trying really hard to control his laughter. He had somehow managed to evade the teacher's eyes during the Geography and Maths classes, but this specific segment of *The Hitchhiker's Guide to the Galaxy* was hilarious. The suppressed laughter came out as a loud snort. He looked up to see if the professor had noticed and decided to at least find out which subject was being taught. He had been so involved in the book, he had lost track of time. Luckily, the professor had not noticed him laughing. As Vikram was about to dive back into the book, he heard Professor Mitra question, 'Who is roll number 64?' Vikram looked around to see who that person was. Nobody was standing up, but he did notice a few pairs of eyes staring at him. Suddenly realizing who roll number 64 was, Vikram stood up.

Professor Mitra stared at the short guy who had suddenly shot up, 'Are you roll number 64?'

Vikram stammered, 'Uh, yes. I think so.'

Professor Mitra raised an eyebrow, 'You think so? Are you sure?'

Vikram took out a register, checked his roll number and blurted, 'Yes sir, I am sure.'

The whole class erupted in laughter as did Professor Mitra. 'Meet me after class,' was all he said to Vikram.

The next twenty minutes passed very slowly. 'Why does sir want to meet me?' was all that was buzzing around in Vikram's head. He jumped from one scenario to another, each worse than the previous one. After chewing his nails for fifteen minutes, the logical part of his brain kicked in—hadn't he written an English exam few days back? And if he remembered correctly, rather than attempting the paper, he had rewritten scenes from his favourite books. *And why had I done that?* Vikram wondered, absentmindedly scrolling through his register. He chanced upon the page where he had copied his favourite writings and recognized a few lines from *The Book Thief* by Markus Zusak. And he remembered the night preceding the English examination vividly.

He had sat with his English books to study, but his thoughts kept going back to the book. He had read about thirty pages of *The Book Thief* and was captivated. The other 520-odd pages were very alluring. Those unread pages were enticing him. He promised himself he would read for just one hour before starting his preparations for the English exam. One hour turned to two, two to four, and four to the hole night. He reached the school next morning, and on seeing the others it hit him that it was an examination day. He had not even opened his book. Looking around he spotted Anant, the class topper, and rushed to him, 'Give me a crash course,' Vikram pleaded.

'What? Now? There are just five minutes left for the exam to start.'

'Please Anant, now!'

'Alright,' said Anant and was able to give Vikram an overview of two of the chapters before the bell rang. As they were going to the examination hall, Anant had one last piece of advice, 'Vikram, bluff as much as you can—use the stuff in the questions to fill up the answer, add a few generic things—and hope for the best.'

Vikram went one step ahead and created his own scenes with the characters. The main answer sheet was filled soon and he asked for a supplement. Anant nodded approvingly. Fifteen minutes later, Vikram asked for another supplement and Anant frowned a little. Forty minutes and two more supplements later, Anant looked incredulous. He himself had used just two supplement sheets and Vikram, who knew nothing, had used four! Exiting the hall, Vikram felt victorious.

Vikram came back to the present with the bell signalling the start of the lunch break. The other students trooped out, but Professor Mitra waited for him. Wondering what was in store for him, Vikram went to the professor's desk and waited for him to say something.

'Do you know why you are here?'

Vikram nodded.

'So what is your excuse?' Professor Mitra asked.

Vikram decided on the truth, 'Sir, I spent the night reading.'

'Obviously not the English textbook,' the professor surmised. 'What were you reading?'

'*The Book Thief*,' Vikram replied.

'The Marcus Zusak book? I've heard it is similar to Anne Frank's *The Diary of a Young Girl*.'

Curious about where the conversation was heading, Vikram

said, 'It is like comparing Kashmiri pulao to Hyderabadi biryani and saying that since both are made of rice, they are similar. Of course there are some common traits in Anne Frank's *The Diary of a Young Girl* and *The Book Thief*—both are based in World War II Germany and the protagonist in both is a young girl, but that is where the similarity ends. In my opinion both are masterpieces, but each in their own right, for very different reasons.'

Professor Mitra's nodding head gave him confidence and Vikram continued, 'One of the best things about the book is that Death is the narrator of the book and starts the book saying, "You are going to die," and yet the book never gets sombre.'

'Interesting. Seems worth a read,' Professor Mitra offered.

'It is not worth a single read, it is worth multiple re-readings,' Vikram was vehement in his opinion.

'I wish you had such drive to read the English textbook,' Professor Mitra brought the train back on track.

Vikram looked down and kept silent.

'Tell me one thing, since when have you been writing?' Professor Mitra asked.

'I don't write, I love reading.'

'You should write, you have a talent for writing—your examination paper is ample proof of that.'

'Sir, do you really think so?'

'I think my judgement about English skills can be trusted. After all I do have over twenty-five years of experience scrutinizing the written word for,' Professor Mitra smiled.

'Thank you, sir.'

'And Vikram, you do know you need to study harder?'

'Yes, sir.'

'Alright Vikram, go on, enjoy your lunch.'

Vikram felt really good, he felt confident. He had earned

praise from his English teacher. English! That rang a bell. Vikram turned and asked the professor, 'Sir, how did I do in the English examination? Will I pass?'

'You will have to wait for a few days like the other students. I think your results will be out by the end of next week,' Professor Mitra replied and his chair toppled over as he stood up.

♦

A few years later...

'Professor Mitra was generous enough to make sure I passed, but did not want me to get overconfident. So he gave me 36 marks out of 100, and the passing mark was 35. His exact words that day were, "I have a soft spot for well-crafted language; other evaluators may not be so kind."' Vikram finished recounting this old tale from his school days.

A voice rang out from among the group of reporters interviewing him, 'In hindsight, not preparing for the examination turned out to be good for you. Actually, very good—a third bestselling novel is something most authors only dream of.'

'I owe it to the confidence instilled in me by Professor Mitra,' Vikram said. 'And indeed, it was an accidental start to a rewarding journey.'

He did not notice when the man sitting in the last row stood up to leave—and the chair toppled over.

Growing Up

ROHINI KEJRIWAL

The frivolous, carefree time of one's early years eventually turns into an enigmatic, tumultuous process that you live out. That process is commonly known as 'growing up'. Becoming an adult is not something everyone looks forward to, tempting as it may sound. You are sitting alone in a corner in your veranda holding a drink in one hand and your lover in your arms. The falling rain is only a distant sound because you are deep in thought about how this is what you had always hoped for—love, money, and happiness. Or is it just part and parcel of the bigger picture?

There is an inward laugh and you realize that though this may be *the* ultimate life, your mind as a child had coloured a completely different painting of what these terms would mean. For a boy, it might have meant that he would be a top cricketer, earning plenty of money and with a wide choice of good-looking girls (probably his own female fan following) to pick his girlfriend (not wife) from. For a girl, it might have been that she would be a respected businesswoman and be financially independent, with a 'cute' boyfriend who loved her. Such were the silly dreams, when a young child's reality was that the two genders hated each other.

The I-Hate-Boys phase came when you read books that told you boys ate snails. Eventually, you grew up and realized that though each boy was worse than the other in terms of the number of snails consumed, that number could not prevent you from having feelings for some of those snail-eaters. The game, Ghar Ghar (role-playing of being in a married household), that you would play with family friends only turned out to be an enactment of what you hoped would reflect in your future. The dressing up, cooking for the one you love, the pretend babies that you looked after with your fake husbands...It is all too embarrassing when one truly realizes the potential of his or her imagination. The wastefulness of your resources would now make you cringe.

Childhood saw a lot of uncalled for demands being met just because 'you are a child, beta, and it is normal for you to want things'. We're talking about the Barbie dolls, the GI Joes, the computer games like Roller Coaster Tycoon, the frequent Lays Chips so that you could increase your Tazo collection, and many other 'objects' that made you momentarily happy. When you grow up, you realize that though those things brought back nice memories, they were never necessities. You look around you and see the much-needed roof above your head, the clothes that are needed to protect you, the food, regardless of what it is, that needs to be consumed by your body. You have learnt that money really does not grow on trees and that you are, contrary to public belief, capable of spending it wisely. You are aware of the choices you have, in terms of what you need and what you don't, of what you would like to do and what you should be doing.

We were very naive and trusting as children. Our minds could be moulded at the convenience of the moulder. Tales of the Big Bad Monster or the Bogeyman would make us eat the green vegetables on our plate so that we didn't end up being eaten by it. The kind Tooth Fairy would make us do idiotic things like putting broken teeth under our pillow and sleeping over those saliva coated, pain-causing things that were once a part of our functional body. Another story fed to us would make us put socks on the ledge with the hope that Santa Claus would think it was a stocking to put gifts in for us.

When, as an 18-year-old, you were out clubbing with your friends on the night of 24th December, you felt a sense of relief that you had found out the truth about those impostors. You were no longer going to be duped into believing that impossible things like the Magic Faraway Tree exist or that an army of evil strawberries was trying to take over the world. At 18, a girl could say that she had legally grown up. Boys had three more years to go for that!

There was always a transparent blindfold that was put over your eyes as a child. It was meant to shield you from the widespread violence that was rampant around you—the communal riots, the murders and the rapes that frequented your city. It was even supposed to prevent you from seeing the human body in its natural form in films like *American Beauty* on nights when your cousins came over to your place for a sleepover with your elder sister. There was always an attempt to preserve your innocence and not let the 'big, bad world' corrupt you. But the corruption, the killings, the cheating, the nudity, the hatred are all imminent realities. They were things that you would never hear about as kids because it was assumed that it was better for you to be ignorant of them. It was probably good to have assumed that on one count at least… Because it sure was nice turning eight and not having communal riots to worry about that day.

But these harsh realities should be slowly introduced as children grow up, so that they are not completely disillusioned when they set out to create an identity for themselves in the world. If not immediately after hearing the news, but eventually, you will learn to accept that a family member who has 'gone away for a long holiday' will not be returning from it. It is better to have light shed on some facts of life rather than being kept completely in the dark.

The brightest place for me was when I was swinging in my

grandmother's garden in her beautiful house in that small, quiet lane in Alipore, Calcutta. I could see the squirrels, and the birds, and the star-fruit…The kamraks that my grandfather would order the gardener to pluck for me before the crows ate them and, then, he'd fondly send them to me knowing that I loved having them with black salt (which never did have a pleasant smell!). I remember the glimpses of grey sky through the leaves swaying in the wind. Bright, powerful glimpses of something unknown but fathomable. I felt something refreshingly new. Freedom—the thing that is so abundant in a way, but hard to truly feel when you've grown up, which is when you are bound to do, say and feel certain things in accordance with the society you are living in. In some situations, you are not even free to think in a particular way because someone who created some silly norm did not approve of such a thought.

You stop what you are doing. You put down the glass in your hand and turn to your lover. He is staring hard at the falling rain and smiling to himself. A smile mirrors across your face on seeing his, and you resume your walk down memory lane. When you were that child that you occasionally let resurface, you trusted people easily. You were gullible and allowed people into your world without giving it a second thought. You would show your art pieces to anyone who was willing to see them. Everybody fascinated you in some way or the other—either because of their enormous head that you deemed would have a lot of brains, or the long beard in which you tried to find chocolate shavings.

As you grew up, you lost loved ones to death, friends to peer pressure, lovers to the fast pace of your life. You experienced loss, fear, love, attachment, sadness, anger, regret, disgust…You accepted that feeling all of those was just a part of living and that you were who you were because of every single experience that you have had. You valued the family and friends who had always been there and lent a helping hand or heard you out when you needed them. Your parents and siblings meant the world to you and you knew that you would do anything to see them happy.

The fights do seem trivial when you think about how lucky you are to have been born into your family. And everyone must be thinking the same thing—*My Daddy is the best Daddy in the whole world.* To each his own, I say. As long as you feel proud of the people you have as your parents and sister, you may be a child at heart or a mature adult, but you will always feel at home. And that is where the heart is.

Essays

Fiction on Campus

SONIA SAFRI

Modern Indian English fiction has seen a distinct surge in the recent past. Breaking away from the usual fads and exploring new sub-genres has become the code of the day... or shall I say, is #trending. Writers nowadays reflect the dreams, aspirations and colours of urban society; concentrating on the contemporary education system, college life, career graphs, social trends, friendship, love, longing, confusion, fear, frustration, aspiration, sacrifice, loneliness, sexual orientation and desires, and the multitude of varied feelings that the urban youth experiences (and is quite vocal about). These writers, experiment with human emotions and churn out brilliant humorous stories, thrillers, chick lit and campus fiction.

Campus fiction ideally revolves around happenings in a college/university/school. Writers take the opportunity to present the academic and personal lives of the characters through different point of views. They describe study pressures, romance, tales of ragging, the academic staff's outlook towards a rebellious and street-smart generation, social outlook and interaction—all key elements of college life that readers have experienced at some point in their lives.

Apart from letting the readers delightfully relive their college days or student life, campus fiction is a true reflection of a major part of society as it exists today. No wonder people find it more appealing. And as someone rightly pointed out—the university/

college is in fact a metaphor for the universe at large.

We all know universities are not just seats of higher academic learning, but also grounds for human emotional growth. Most writers pen their first-hand experiences, sometimes exaggerated and comically tuned, endorsing authenticity to an extent. And this is keeping in mind a majority of the readers today who prefer a light read maybe over coffee breaks, or while travelling, or just for pleasure. The feeling of déjà vu and nostalgia while reading about college life and the antics of the characters of the story makes such stories hands-down winners.

There have been a number of novels set against the backdrop of IIT (and we all know where and how that began) but Abhijit Bhaduri's *Mediocre But Arrogant* set in the 'Management Institute of Jamshedpur' brought management institutes to the limelight and to our bookshelves. The book smartly portrays two years of a student's life in a management institute. The characters and the setting were absolutely real and relatable, and it honestly did not come across as a deliberate attempt to impress the readers.

Others worth mentioning include Ritesh Sharma and Neeraj Pahlajani's *Joker in the Pack* set in the IIM (Indian Institute of Management) campus and Karan Bajaj's *Keep Off the Grass. Keep Off the Grass* saw Samrat (the protagonist) leave his life and career as an investment banker in New York and come to India to study at the IIM. *Joker in the Pack* is a tongue-in-cheek story about life at the IIM and beyond. It inspires youngsters to seek admission to the IIMs and live their 'student life' to the fullest while bringing nostalgia amongst the alumni.

Amitabha Bagchi's *Above Average* revolves around a boy's dreams torn between IIT and joining a rock band. Written in uncomplicated and simple prose, the book depicts how life is not always the same. People either get over-ambitious or remain underachievers. They set goals/aspirations that are not always achievable. Arindam too finds himself in such a situation where he reflects on his life's achievements and tries to reassess them.

Anirban Bose's *Bombay Rains, Bombay Girls* is beautifully set in a medical school. Adi comes to Bombay from a small town to study medicine. Stumbling between the principles of a doctor's life and friendship, Adi gets a grip on himself down the line.

Soma Das' *Sumthing of a Mocktale*, based on the politics and jeans-jhola-kurta culture of JNU, comes as close to reality as it can. Misfits, social and popular butterflies, geeks, nerds, dopers, lovers— you are sure to find all the characters easy to relate to. Life takes a full circle as the main characters find themselves maturing and evolving into responsible adults who discover that they can neither leave nor live in JNU.

Srividya Natarajan's *No Onions Nor Garlic*, set in the University of Chennai, takes a shot at Tam-Brahms (Tamilians) and Indians at large. This satirical novel is about the caste system in the country and, though a bit exaggerated, it is still pretty hilarious.

Sudeep Chakravarti's *Tin Fish* is a school story set in the elite Mayo College boarding school of Rajasthan. Anyone who has lived in a boarding school is sure to relive their experiences once again on reading this book. It revolves around teachers, principals, girls, friends, punishments, praises and the whole jazz that comes with hostel life. It is not very in-depth but a fun read about the Indian boarding school. Kaushik Sircar's *Three Makes a Crowd* depicts hostel life at Dehradun's Rashtriya Indian Military College.

Of late, glimpses of college life and blossoming love were seen in Shaiju Mathew's *Knocked Up*, where the notorious trio reminds us of our college days. Ahmed Faiyaz's *Love, Life And All That Jazz* and *Another Chance* are a way of depicting college love and friendship standing the test of time and evolving into mature

234*Urban Shots Down the Road

love stories.

But come to think of it, Ruskin Bond and R. K. Narayan should be hailed as the trendsetters, since most of their work revolved around stories from school. In fact, if I remember right, R. K. Narayan's *Swami and Friends* and *The Bachelor Of Arts* were amongst the very first Indian campus fiction novels in English.

Readers associate with the characters and the storyline, (given the simple language) an adequate usage of Hinglish terms and phrases, the realistic situations and the tone of the storyteller. The beauty lies in the presentation of the writer. No wonder campus fiction, especially, is an instant hit amongst the masses. Yes, due credit goes to the fair pricing and innovative marketing strategies that help to a great extent in reaching out.

As long as the story is not drab, boring and colourless and exudes freshness and humour, of course, campus fiction will not lose lustre soon.

Bollywood on Campus

ASEEM RASTOGI

Students going gaga over the new girl in college (*Ishq Vishq*). The hero wooing her with a song (*Pyar Kiya Toh Darna Kya*). His friends, who are nothing but sidekicks, break into a jig at every given opportunity (*Dil*). Students who wear everything from designer micro-minis to baggy jeans (*Pyaar Mein Kabhi Kabhi*). Teachers who seem like comic caricatures plugged into the scene (*Paathshala* and *Taare Zameen Par*). Is this what campus life is all about?

For a hard-core critic, such movies would seem an utter waste of time. But for the masses, did I hear someone say paisa-vasool entertainment?

While Bollywood has been on campus for years, I would like to reflect on cinema that I've grown up with, which has inspired and entertained us over the past two decades—some flicks like *3 Idiots* had stars, while others like *Udaan* didn't; some discussed campus politics, while others challenged the age-old system of learning by rote; some became hits, while others flopped. But what was common was the relentless hard work that went into giving us a small peek into college life.

Wooing a girl, the competing spirit, inter-college rivalry—*Jo Jeeta Wohi Sikandar* (*JJWS*) had it all. Released eighteen years ago, its innocence and fun is still fresh. Even today, while listening to 'Pehla Nasha', one thinks about one's girlfriend or boyfriend, and is compelled to relive one's years in school/college.

If *JJWS* lightens your mood, both *Kuch Kuch Hota Hai* and *Jaane Tu Ya Jaane Na* get you nostalgic about your college flame. In the world of romance, clichés rule. For all the fun and banter between college friends, for the chemistry between the lead pair and the great times at college, these movies make you smile.

Never believed in love? Found your true love every time? Weren't interested in romance? Confused in life? I am sure most of us would have experienced such situations in our lives before. *Dil Chahta Hai* and *Wake Up Sid* are about all this and more. The pranks played on friends; the travails of careers; the quirks of fate and destiny; the importance of love and life; both these movies make you remember your gang of friends at school or college.

Can any discussion on romance leave out *Mohabbatein*? A school aptly named 'Gurukul', headed by the strictest disciplinarian, with a quirky anti-romance policy: that's what you call make-believe cinema. The clash between love and discipline, the passion for a lost love, the blossoming love between the three couples, and the way the youth unite to fight the oppressor makes for a compelling tale. As for studies, who really cares?

Shah Rukh Khan going to college at the ripe old age of 40 to protect and re-establish relations with his half-brother, Zayed Khan, and stepmother seems like a masala flick at the outset. A college where a super-hot Sushmita Sen is a teacher and makes heads turn in her chiffon saris, where prom nights are as common as getting a girl—your dream college, isn't it? *Main Hoon Na* is like a walk down memory lane.

Is college life only about falling in love, proposing and having fun with friends? Are campuses only meant for singing, dancing and entertainment?

Rockford was probably one of the most realistic movies depicting life at an all-male boarding school. Bullying and ragging ran rampant, teachers were seen asking for sexual favours, students had crushes on teachers, but it had its heart in the right place.

A movie which may have been well ahead of its time, *Kya Kehna* portrayed a pregnant college student overcoming the disdain of society to live a life of respect. In accepting this role, Preity Zinta went on to inspire women facing similar situations.

In other break-away movies, characters played by both Darsheel Safary and Hrithik Roshan were made fun of because of their looks, the way they spoke and their poor academic records. On one hand, *Taare Zameen Par* was an inspirational flick about realising one's potential, while on the other, *Koi Mil Gaya* was a crowd puller with aliens and the like. But both of them depicted the difficulties faced by people with disabilities without any bias whatsoever. On another tangent, Amitabh Bachchan as a school kid, Auro, in *Paa* made people smile and cry at the same time.

Dil Dosti Etc. takes us into the life of two individuals, as different as chalk and cheese, with a similar ambition. Imaad Shah is rich and aimless and decides to sleep with three different girls before the university election results. Shreyas Talpade, on the other hand, is a middle-class Bihari who campaigns for his candidature with violence against others. It is the story of the liberal elite with no strings attached versus the conservative middle-class.

While talking about politics, the two movies that come to one's mind are *Haasil* and *Rang De Basanti*. While Irfan Khan uses every wrong way in the book to do the right thing, Atul Kulkarni believes that fundamentalism is the way forward. Irfan misuses his friends to achieve what he sets out for, but Atul lives the character of Ram Prasad Bismil, and finally realises that one has to take to violent means to make a difference.

Breaking the conventional myths of doing things in a particular way, *3 Idiots* and *Munnabhai MBBS* showed us that we can be creative and still succeed in this society.

While Munnabhai treats his patients with his characteristic jaadoo ki jhappis (magical hugs), Rancho makes a mockery of an educational system which involves learning by rote. Munnabhai, as a medical student, tries to cheer up everyone with his empathy and care, while Rancho works his way by encouraging creativity and out-of-the-box thinking.

In *Udaan*, when Rajat Barmecha is thrown out of his boarding school, little does he realise the circumstances he will have to face at home. He encounters a father who hasn't bothered about him for eight years, and a half-brother who he never knew existed. Despite aspiring to become a writer, he agrees to pursue engineering when his father forces him. He faces the physical abuse his father inflicts on him and realises that his brother had to go through the same. It depicts situations that still exist in small towns in India, where an engineering or management degree is seen as the passport to a good life, and children are lined up at an early age to run the rat race. It raises some important questions. If one's parents don't support a child, how will he face the world? Does *Udaan* ring a bell in your child or you as a parent?

From candy-floss romance to movies that inspire you like *Rang de Basanti, Udaan* and *Taare Zameen Par,* from ragging in colleges to protesting against the conventional ways of learning à la 3 *Idiots,* our movies seem to have gone through a sea change in the kind of campus life they depict. I, for one, look forward to the next blockbuster based on a campus! Circuit goes to school, what say?